·THE BLUECOATS·

COSSACK CIRCUS

ARTWORK: WILLY LAMBIL   **SCRIPT: RAOUL CAUVIN**

9th CINEBOOK
The 9th Art Publisher

Original title: Les Tuniques Bleues – Les Bleus tournent cosaques
Original edition: © Dupuis, 1977
by Lambil & Cauvin
www.dupuis.com
All rights reserved
English translation: © 2018 Cinebook Ltd
Translator: Jerome Saincantin
Editor: Erica Olson Jeffrey
Lettering and text layout: Design Amorandi
Printed in Spain by EGEDSA
This edition first published in Great Britain in 2018 by
Cinebook Ltd
56 Beech Avenue
Canterbury, Kent
CT4 7TA
www.cinebook.com
A CIP catalogue record for this book
is available from the British Library
ISBN 978-1-84918-383-3

9th CINEBOOK
The 9th Art Publisher

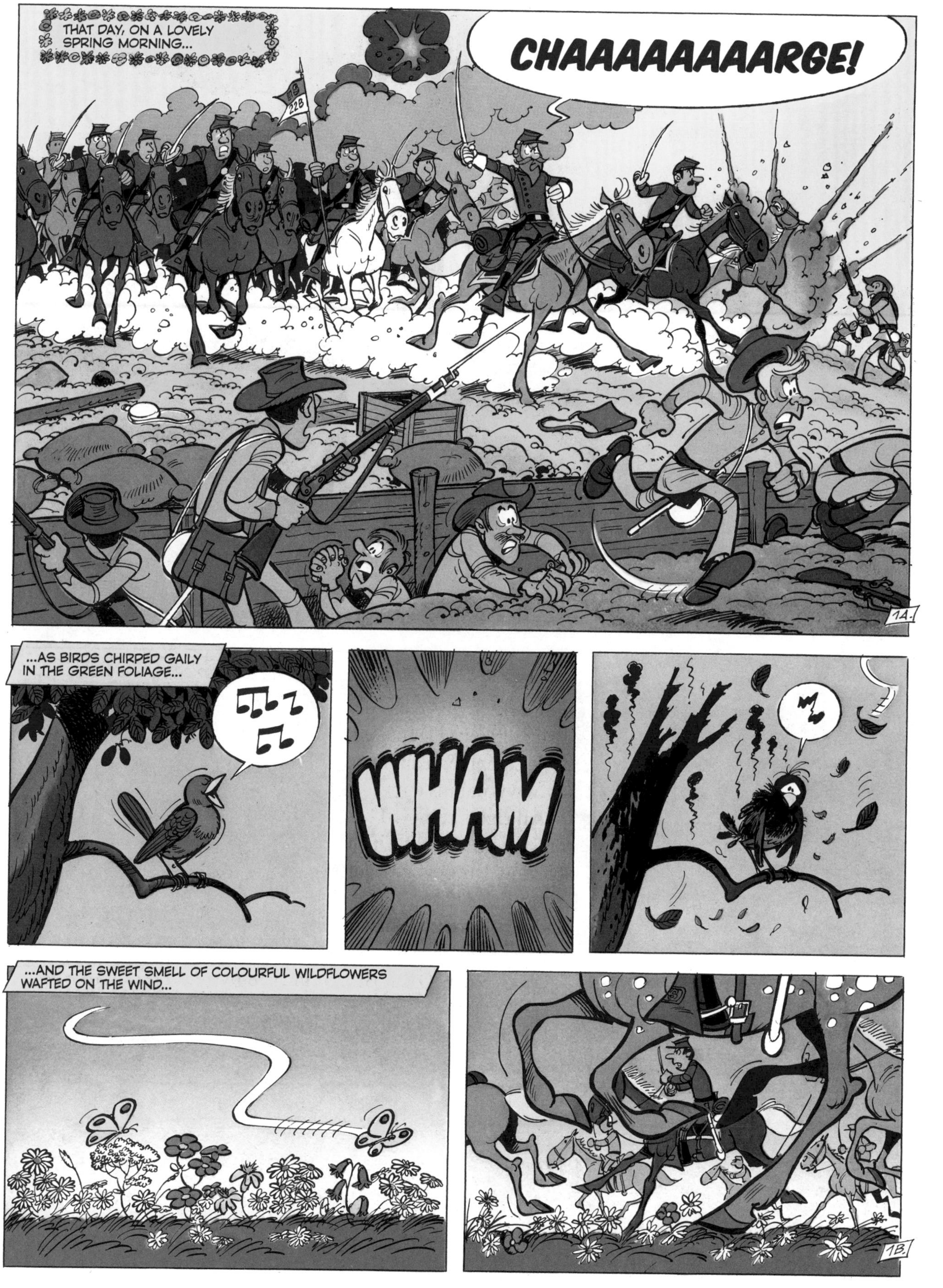
THAT DAY, ON A LOVELY SPRING MORNING...
CHAAAAAAAARGE!
...AS BIRDS CHIRPED GAILY IN THE GREEN FOLIAGE...
WHAM
...AND THE SWEET SMELL OF COLOURFUL WILDFLOWERS WAFTED ON THE WIND...

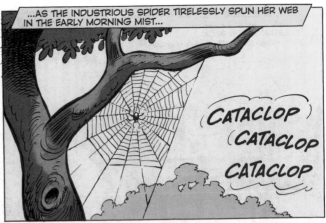

...AS THE INDUSTRIOUS SPIDER TIRELESSLY SPUN HER WEB IN THE EARLY MORNING MIST...

CATACLOP

CATACLOP

CATACLOP

?!

2A.

I'M SICK OF THIS! I'M SO SICK OF THIS!

BLUTCH! WHAT HAPPENED? HAVE YOU BEEN INJURED?

NO, SARGE! I TOOK A SPIDER TO THE RIGHT EYE!

THAT'S THE BEST YOU COULD COME UP WITH TO AVOID CHARGING, YOU LITTLE COWARD?

IF YOU WANT TO KEEP YOUR LEFT EYE HEALTHY, I SUGGEST YOU GET BACK ON YOUR HORSE!

HMM? WHAT HORSE?...

I MUST SAY, THIS IS THE FIRST TIME I'LL CHARGE IN A SERGEANT'S ARMS!

DON'T GET ANY IDEAS, YOU NITWIT! I SAID YOU'D CHARGE, AND SO YOU WILL!

2B.

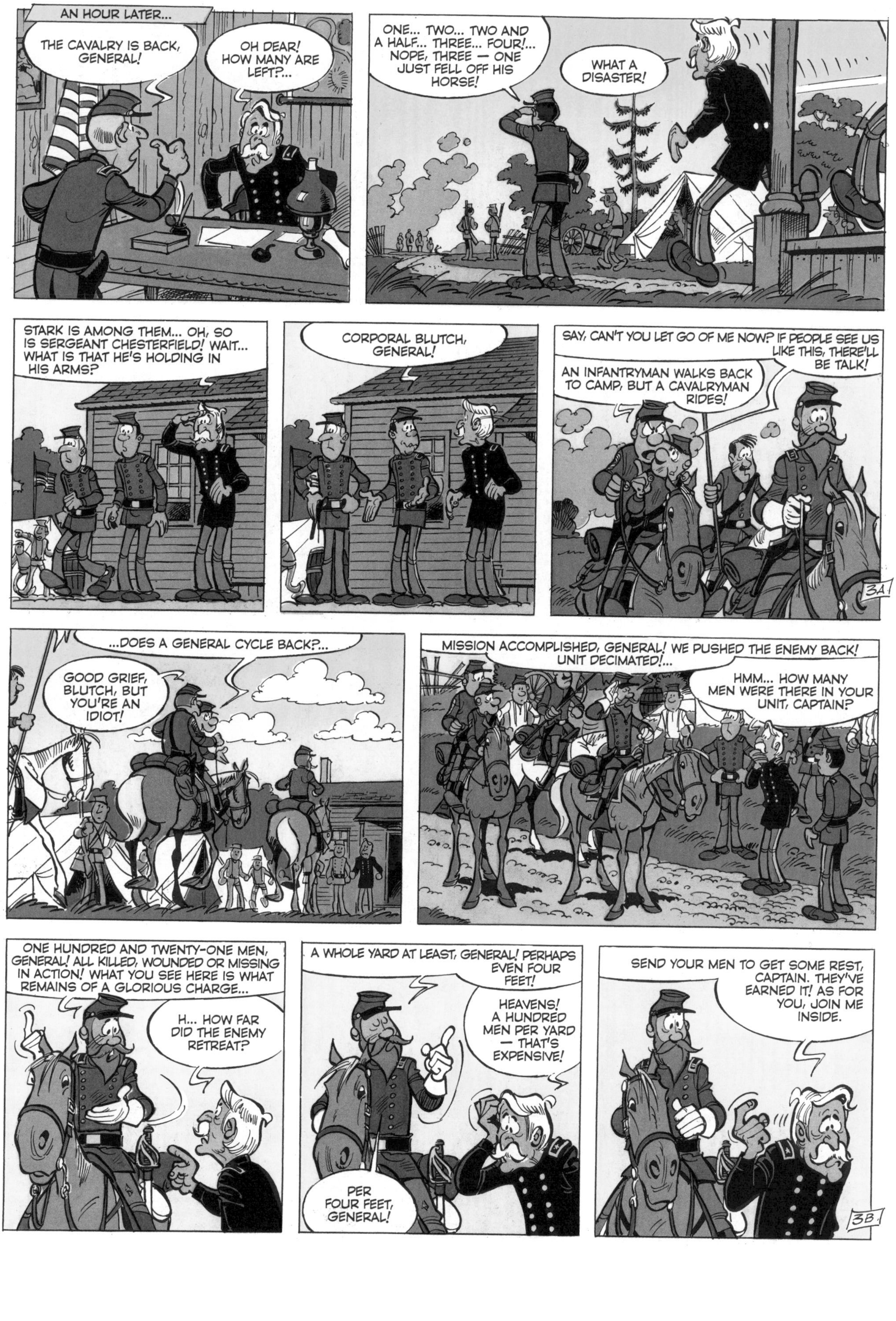

AN HOUR LATER...
THE CAVALRY IS BACK, GENERAL!
OH DEAR! HOW MANY ARE LEFT?...
ONE... TWO... TWO AND A HALF... THREE... FOUR!... NOPE, THREE — ONE JUST FELL OFF HIS HORSE!
WHAT A DISASTER!
STARK IS AMONG THEM... OH, SO IS SERGEANT CHESTERFIELD! WAIT... WHAT IS THAT HE'S HOLDING IN HIS ARMS?
CORPORAL BLUTCH, GENERAL!
SAY, CAN'T YOU LET GO OF ME NOW? IF PEOPLE SEE US LIKE THIS, THERE'LL BE TALK!
AN INFANTRYMAN WALKS BACK TO CAMP, BUT A CAVALRYMAN RIDES!
3A
...DOES A GENERAL CYCLE BACK?...
GOOD GRIEF, BLUTCH, BUT YOU'RE AN IDIOT!
MISSION ACCOMPLISHED, GENERAL! WE PUSHED THE ENEMY BACK! UNIT DECIMATED!...
HMM... HOW MANY MEN WERE THERE IN YOUR UNIT, CAPTAIN?
ONE HUNDRED AND TWENTY-ONE MEN, GENERAL! ALL KILLED, WOUNDED OR MISSING IN ACTION! WHAT YOU SEE HERE IS WHAT REMAINS OF A GLORIOUS CHARGE...
H... HOW FAR DID THE ENEMY RETREAT?
A WHOLE YARD AT LEAST, GENERAL! PERHAPS EVEN FOUR FEET!
HEAVENS! A HUNDRED MEN PER YARD — THAT'S EXPENSIVE!
PER FOUR FEET, GENERAL!
SEND YOUR MEN TO GET SOME REST, CAPTAIN. THEY'VE EARNED IT! AS FOR YOU, JOIN ME INSIDE.
3B

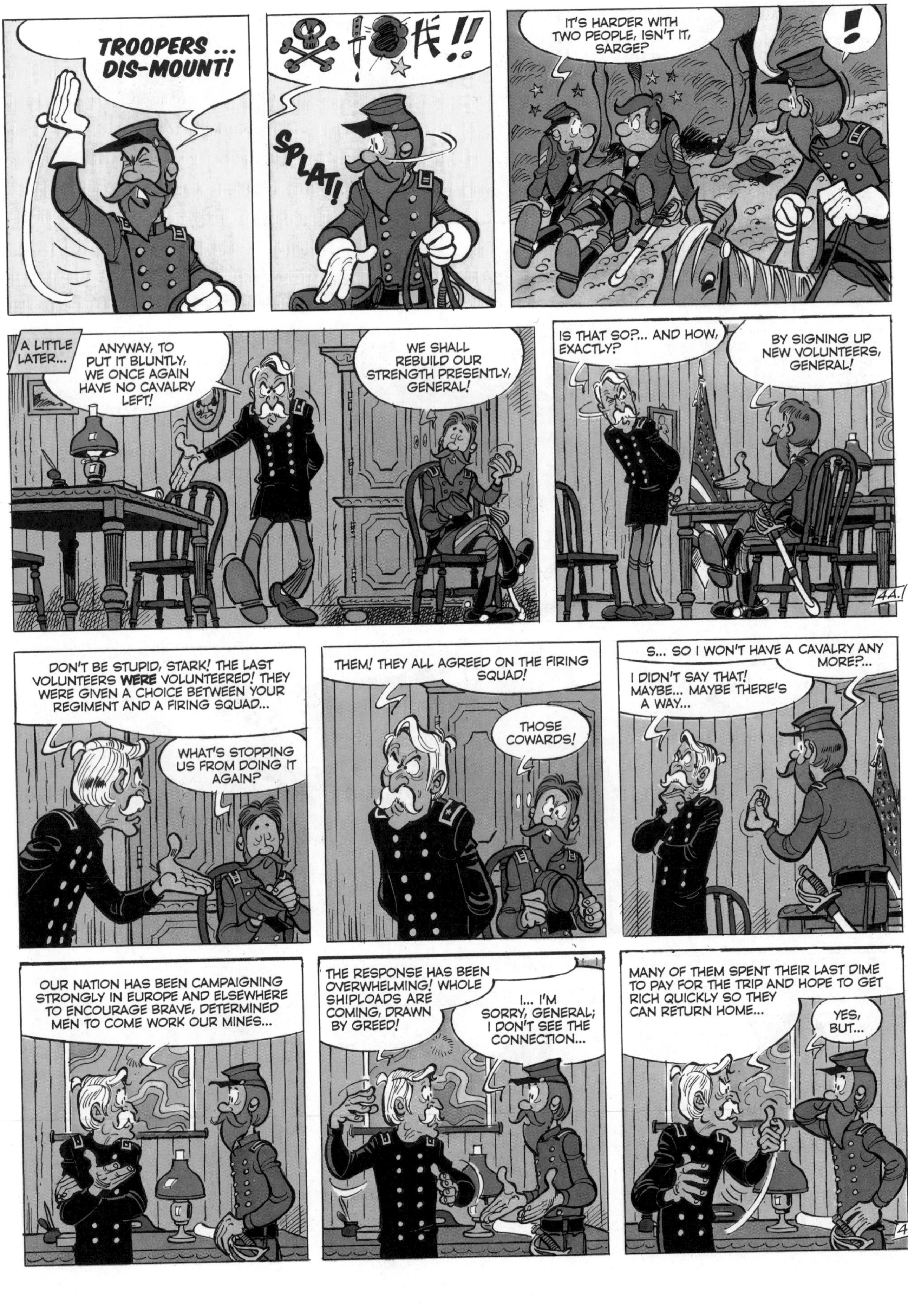
TROOPERS ... DIS-MOUNT!
SPLAT!
!!
IT'S HARDER WITH TWO PEOPLE, ISN'T IT, SARGE?
!
A LITTLE LATER...
ANYWAY, TO PUT IT BLUNTLY, WE ONCE AGAIN HAVE NO CAVALRY LEFT!
WE SHALL REBUILD OUR STRENGTH PRESENTLY, GENERAL!
IS THAT SO?... AND HOW, EXACTLY?
BY SIGNING UP NEW VOLUNTEERS, GENERAL!
DON'T BE STUPID, STARK! THE LAST VOLUNTEERS **WERE** VOLUNTEERED! THEY WERE GIVEN A CHOICE BETWEEN YOUR REGIMENT AND A FIRING SQUAD...
WHAT'S STOPPING US FROM DOING IT AGAIN?
THEM! THEY ALL AGREED ON THE FIRING SQUAD!
THOSE COWARDS!
S... SO I WON'T HAVE A CAVALRY ANY MORE?...
I DIDN'T SAY THAT! MAYBE... MAYBE THERE'S A WAY...
OUR NATION HAS BEEN CAMPAIGNING STRONGLY IN EUROPE AND ELSEWHERE TO ENCOURAGE BRAVE, DETERMINED MEN TO COME WORK OUR MINES...
THE RESPONSE HAS BEEN OVERWHELMING! WHOLE SHIPLOADS ARE COMING, DRAWN BY GREED!
I... I'M SORRY, GENERAL; I DON'T SEE THE CONNECTION...
MANY OF THEM SPENT THEIR LAST DIME TO PAY FOR THE TRIP AND HOPE TO GET RICH QUICKLY SO THEY CAN RETURN HOME...
YES, BUT...

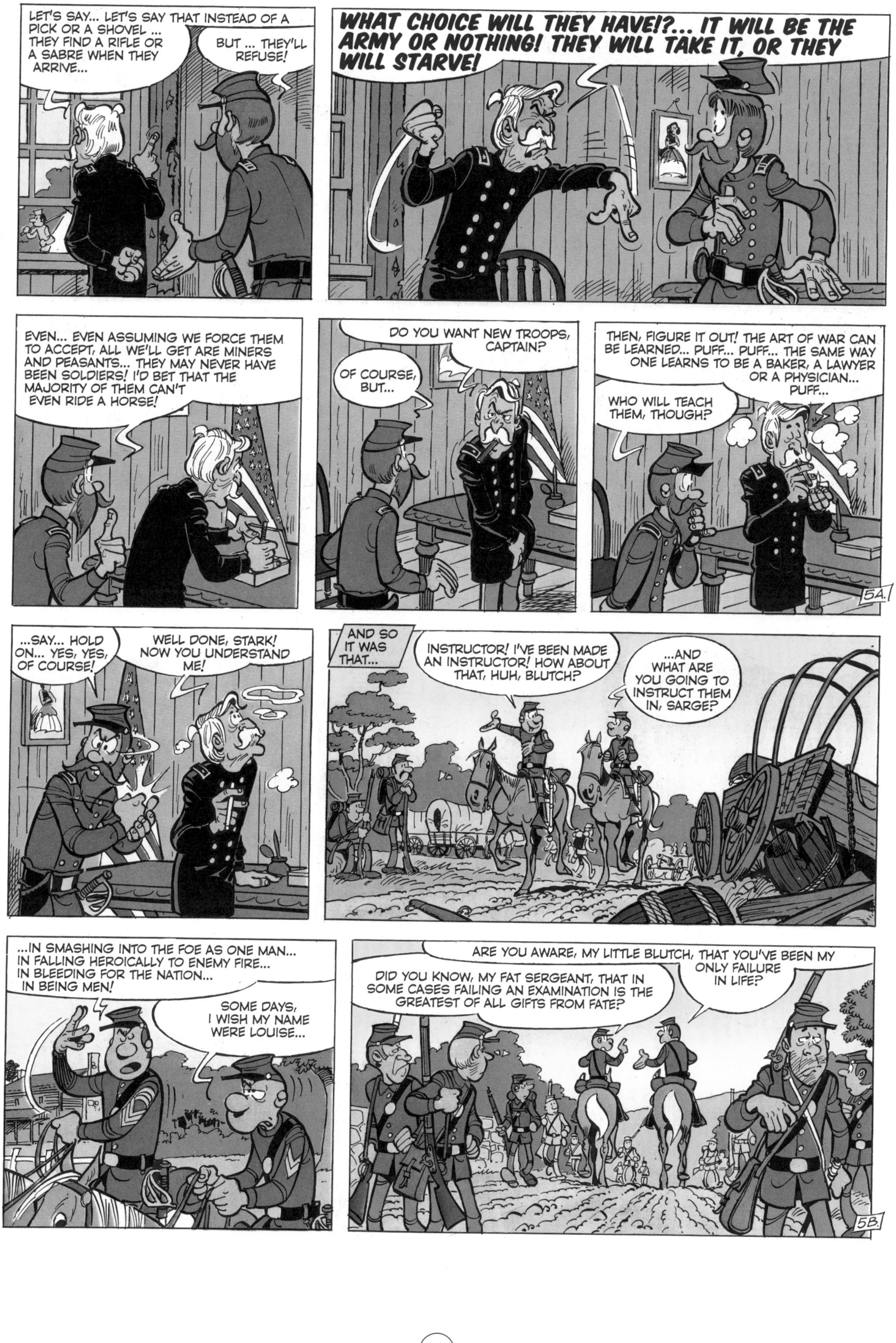
LET'S SAY... LET'S SAY THAT INSTEAD OF A PICK OR A SHOVEL ... THEY FIND A RIFLE OR A SABRE WHEN THEY ARRIVE...
BUT ... THEY'LL REFUSE!
WHAT CHOICE WILL THEY HAVE!?... IT WILL BE THE ARMY OR NOTHING! THEY WILL TAKE IT, OR THEY WILL STARVE!
EVEN... EVEN ASSUMING WE FORCE THEM TO ACCEPT, ALL WE'LL GET ARE MINERS AND PEASANTS... THEY MAY NEVER HAVE BEEN SOLDIERS! I'D BET THAT THE MAJORITY OF THEM CAN'T EVEN RIDE A HORSE!
DO YOU WANT NEW TROOPS, CAPTAIN?
OF COURSE, BUT...
THEN, FIGURE IT OUT! THE ART OF WAR CAN BE LEARNED... PUFF... PUFF... THE SAME WAY ONE LEARNS TO BE A BAKER, A LAWYER OR A PHYSICIAN... PUFF...
WHO WILL TEACH THEM, THOUGH?
...SAY... HOLD ON... YES, YES, OF COURSE!
WELL DONE, STARK! NOW YOU UNDERSTAND ME!
AND SO IT WAS THAT...
INSTRUCTOR! I'VE BEEN MADE AN INSTRUCTOR! HOW ABOUT THAT, HUH, BLUTCH?
...AND WHAT ARE YOU GOING TO INSTRUCT THEM IN, SARGE?
...IN SMASHING INTO THE FOE AS ONE MAN... IN FALLING HEROICALLY TO ENEMY FIRE... IN BLEEDING FOR THE NATION... IN BEING MEN!
SOME DAYS, I WISH MY NAME WERE LOUISE...
ARE YOU AWARE, MY LITTLE BLUTCH, THAT YOU'VE BEEN MY ONLY FAILURE IN LIFE?
DID YOU KNOW, MY FAT SERGEANT, THAT IN SOME CASES FAILING AN EXAMINATION IS THE GREATEST OF ALL GIFTS FROM FATE?

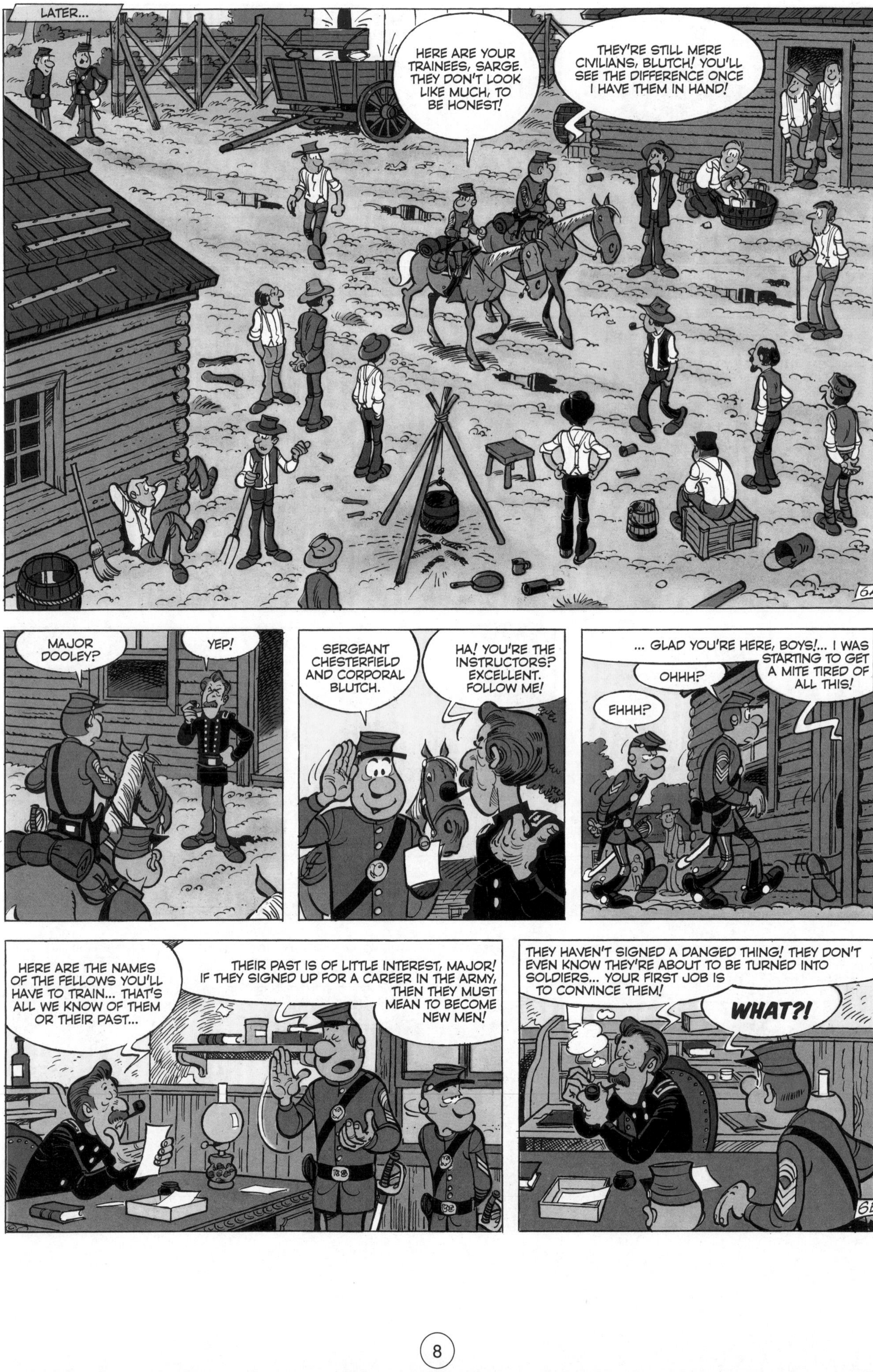
LATER...
HERE ARE YOUR TRAINEES, SARGE. THEY DON'T LOOK LIKE MUCH, TO BE HONEST!
THEY'RE STILL MERE CIVILIANS, BLUTCH! YOU'LL SEE THE DIFFERENCE ONCE I HAVE THEM IN HAND!
6A.
MAJOR DOOLEY?
YEP!
SERGEANT CHESTERFIELD AND CORPORAL BLUTCH.
HA! YOU'RE THE INSTRUCTORS? EXCELLENT. FOLLOW ME!
... GLAD YOU'RE HERE, BOYS!... I WAS STARTING TO GET A MITE TIRED OF ALL THIS!
OHHH?
EHHH?
HERE ARE THE NAMES OF THE FELLOWS YOU'LL HAVE TO TRAIN... THAT'S ALL WE KNOW OF THEM OR THEIR PAST...
THEIR PAST IS OF LITTLE INTEREST, MAJOR! IF THEY SIGNED UP FOR A CAREER IN THE ARMY, THEN THEY MUST MEAN TO BECOME NEW MEN!
THEY HAVEN'T SIGNED A DANGED THING! THEY DON'T EVEN KNOW THEY'RE ABOUT TO BE TURNED INTO SOLDIERS... YOUR FIRST JOB IS TO CONVINCE THEM!
WHAT?!
6B.

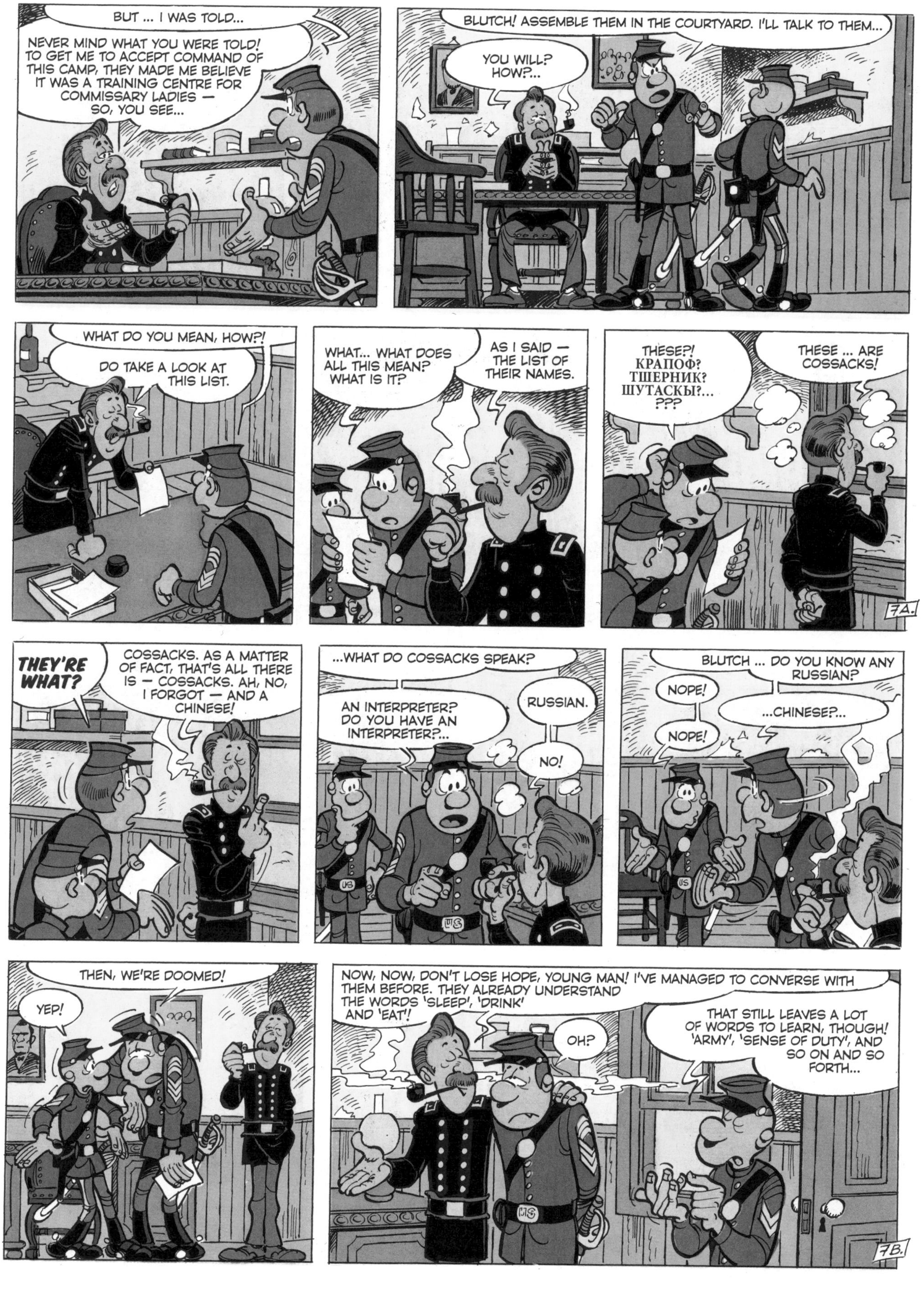
BUT ... I WAS TOLD...
NEVER MIND WHAT YOU WERE TOLD! TO GET ME TO ACCEPT COMMAND OF THIS CAMP, THEY MADE ME BELIEVE IT WAS A TRAINING CENTRE FOR COMMISSARY LADIES — SO, YOU SEE...
BLUTCH! ASSEMBLE THEM IN THE COURTYARD. I'LL TALK TO THEM...
YOU WILL? HOW?...
WHAT DO YOU MEAN, HOW?!
DO TAKE A LOOK AT THIS LIST.
WHAT... WHAT DOES ALL THIS MEAN? WHAT IS IT?
AS I SAID — THE LIST OF THEIR NAMES.
THESE?! КРАПОФ? ТШЕРНИК? ШУТАСКЫ?... ???
THESE ... ARE COSSACKS!
THEY'RE WHAT?
COSSACKS. AS A MATTER OF FACT, THAT'S ALL THERE IS — COSSACKS. AH, NO, I FORGOT — AND A CHINESE!
...WHAT DO COSSACKS SPEAK?
RUSSIAN.
AN INTERPRETER? DO YOU HAVE AN INTERPRETER?...
NO!
BLUTCH ... DO YOU KNOW ANY RUSSIAN?
NOPE!
...CHINESE?...
NOPE!
THEN, WE'RE DOOMED!
YEP!
NOW, NOW, DON'T LOSE HOPE, YOUNG MAN! I'VE MANAGED TO CONVERSE WITH THEM BEFORE. THEY ALREADY UNDERSTAND THE WORDS 'SLEEP', 'DRINK' AND 'EAT'!
OH?
THAT STILL LEAVES A LOT OF WORDS TO LEARN, THOUGH! 'ARMY', 'SENSE OF DUTY', AND SO ON AND SO FORTH...

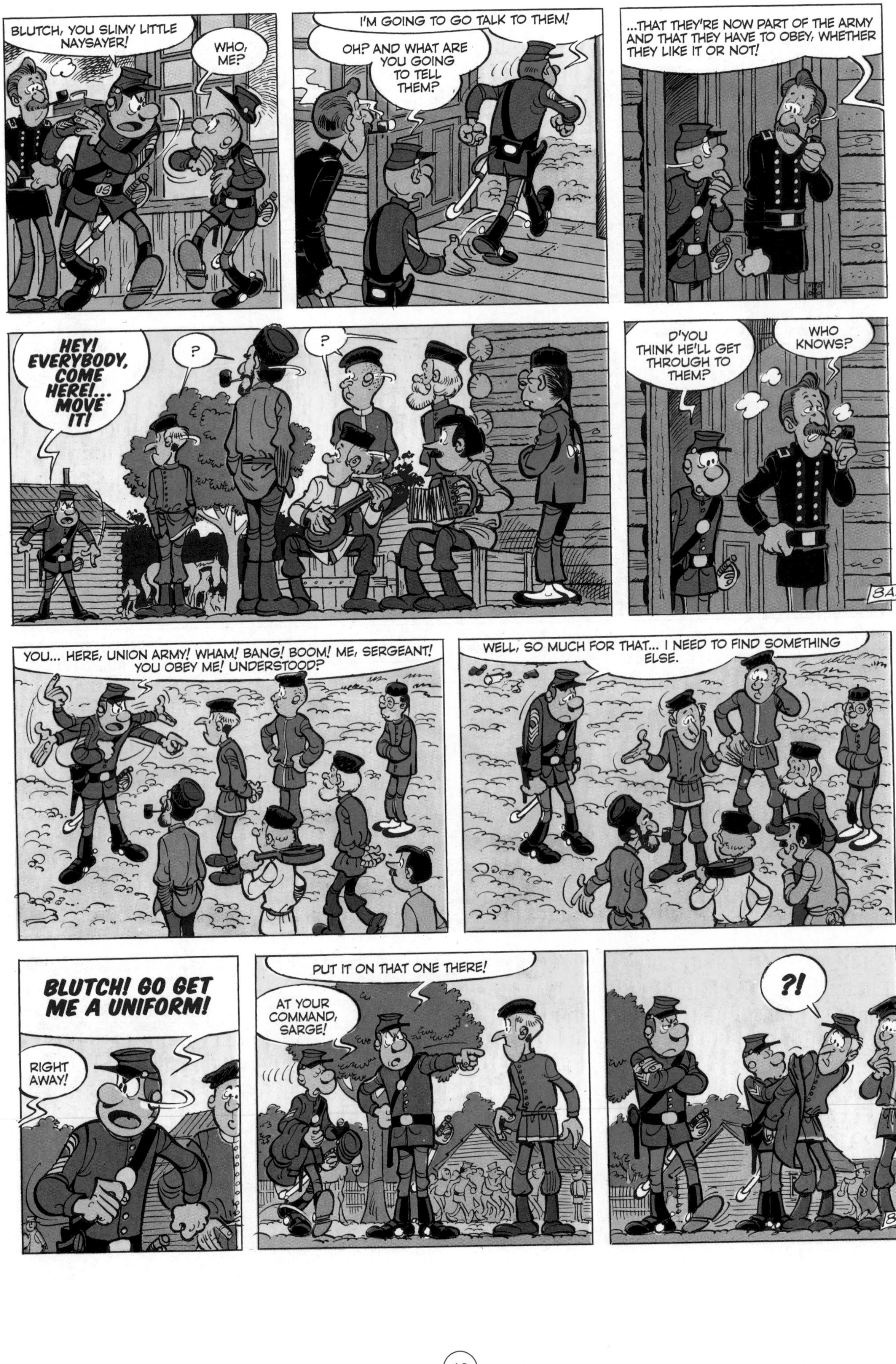
BLUTCH, YOU SLIMY LITTLE NAYSAYER!
WHO, ME?
I'M GOING TO GO TALK TO THEM!
OH? AND WHAT ARE YOU GOING TO TELL THEM?
...THAT THEY'RE NOW PART OF THE ARMY AND THAT THEY HAVE TO OBEY, WHETHER THEY LIKE IT OR NOT!
HEY! EVERYBODY, COME HERE!... MOVE IT!
?
?
D'YOU THINK HE'LL GET THROUGH TO THEM?
WHO KNOWS?
YOU... HERE, UNION ARMY! WHAM! BANG! BOOM! ME, SERGEANT! YOU OBEY ME! UNDERSTOOD?
WELL, SO MUCH FOR THAT... I NEED TO FIND SOMETHING ELSE.
BLUTCH! GO GET ME A UNIFORM!
RIGHT AWAY!
PUT IT ON THAT ONE THERE!
AT YOUR COMMAND, SARGE!
?!

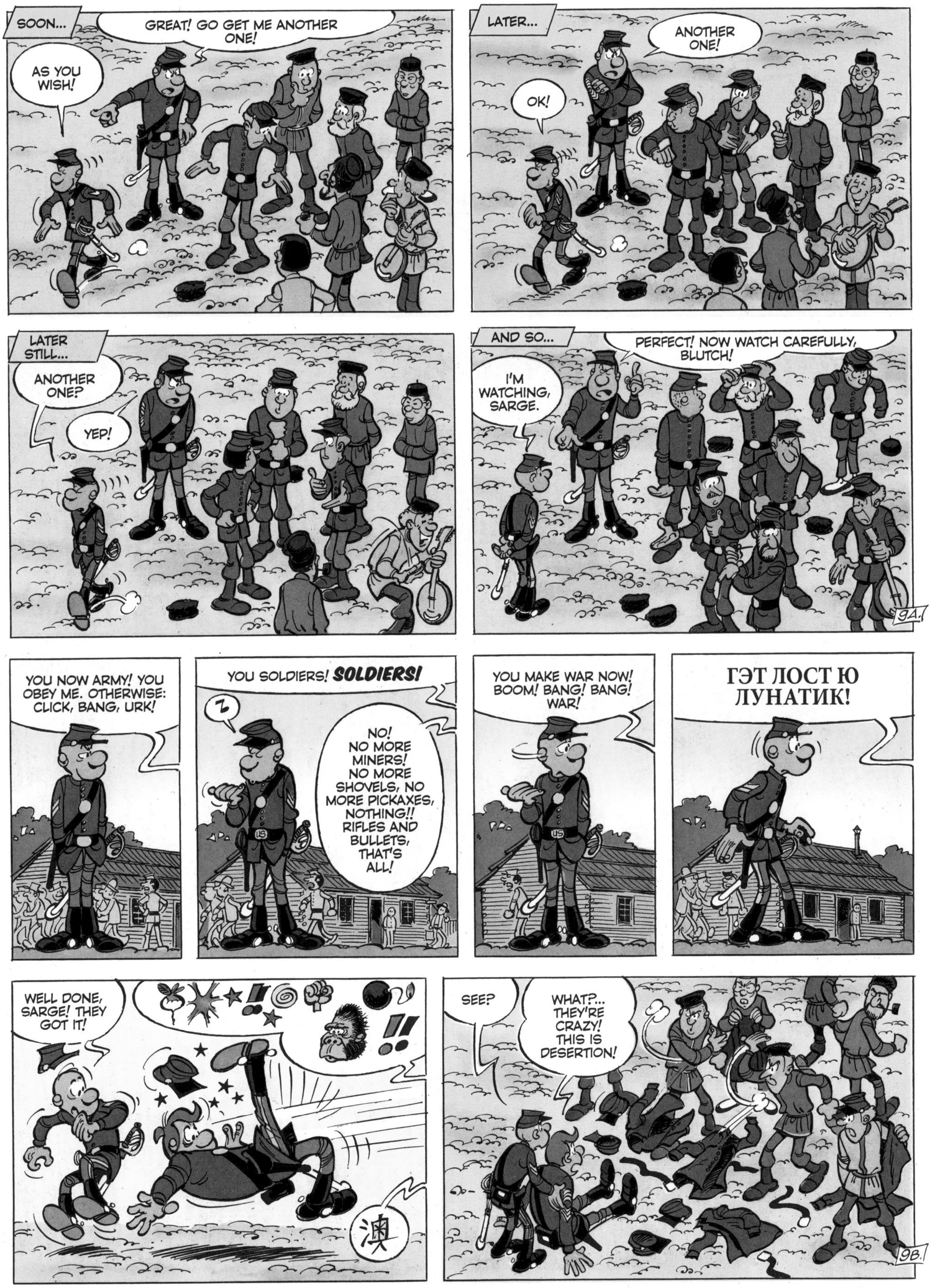

SOON...
GREAT! GO GET ME ANOTHER ONE!
AS YOU WISH!
LATER...
ANOTHER ONE!
OK!
LATER STILL...
ANOTHER ONE?
YEP!
AND SO...
PERFECT! NOW WATCH CAREFULLY, BLUTCH!
I'M WATCHING, SARGE.
YOU NOW ARMY! YOU OBEY ME. OTHERWISE: CLICK, BANG, URK!
YOU SOLDIERS! SOLDIERS!
NO! NO MORE MINERS! NO MORE SHOVELS, NO MORE PICKAXES, NOTHING!! RIFLES AND BULLETS, THAT'S ALL!
YOU MAKE WAR NOW! BOOM! BANG! BANG! WAR!
ГЭТ ЛОСТ Ю ЛУНАТИК!
WELL DONE, SARGE! THEY GOT IT!
澳
SEE?
WHAT?... THEY'RE CRAZY! THIS IS DESERTION!

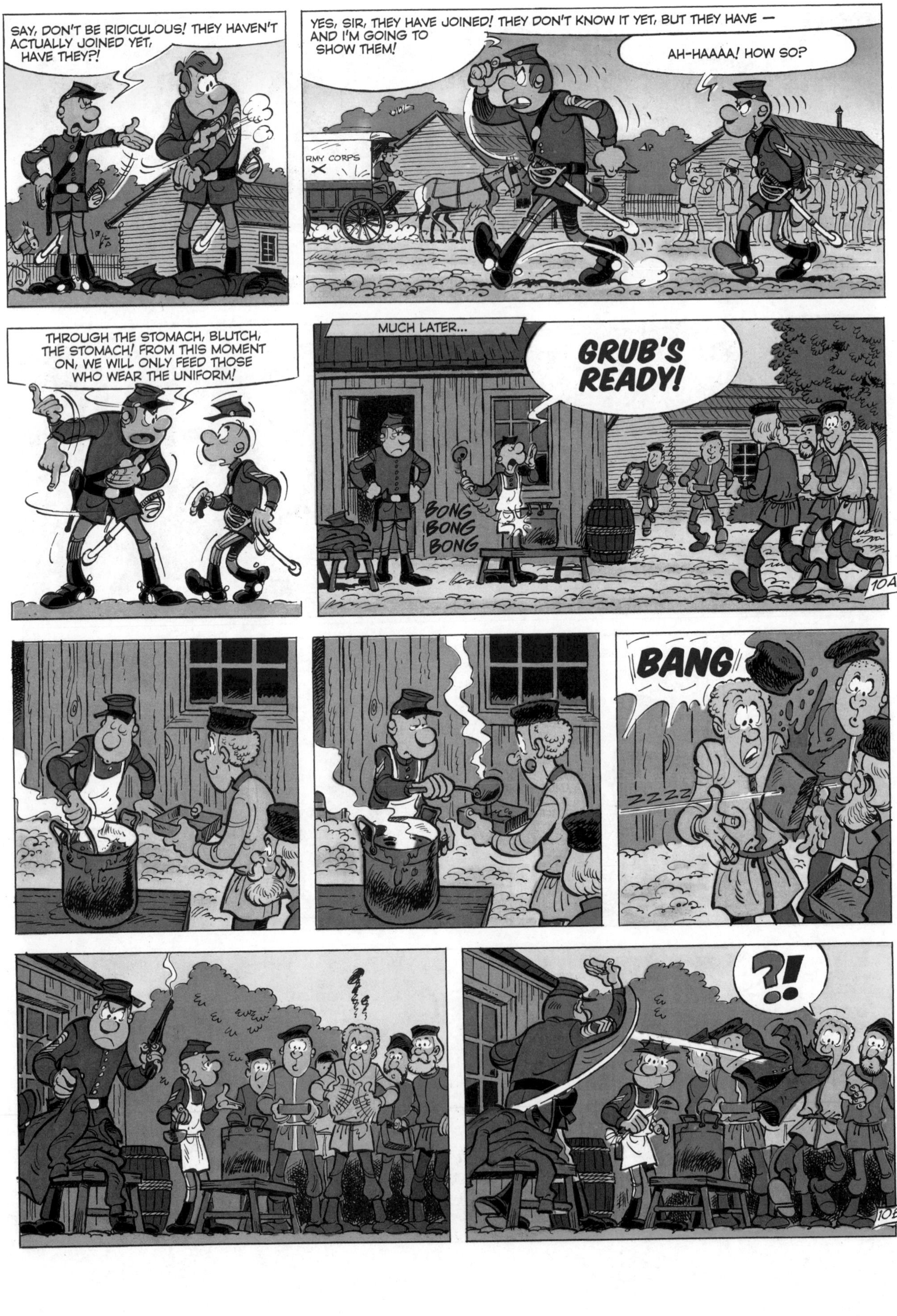
SAY, DON'T BE RIDICULOUS! THEY HAVEN'T ACTUALLY JOINED YET, HAVE THEY?!
YES, SIR, THEY HAVE JOINED! THEY DON'T KNOW IT YET, BUT THEY HAVE — AND I'M GOING TO SHOW THEM!
AH-HAAAA! HOW SO?
RMY CORPS
THROUGH THE STOMACH, BLUTCH, THE STOMACH! FROM THIS MOMENT ON, WE WILL ONLY FEED THOSE WHO WEAR THE UNIFORM!
MUCH LATER...
GRUB'S READY!
BONG BONG BONG
10A
BANG
ZZZZ
?!
10B

KLANG

DOESN'T SEEM TO BE WORKING TOO WELL, EH, SARGE!

PATIENCE, BLUTCH!

IN A DAY OR TWO, THEIR STOMACHS WILL BE AS EMPTY AS YOUR HEAD, AND THEY'LL COME BEG ME TO BE ALLOWED TO WEAR THE UNIFORM!

...ASSUMING YOU'RE NOT FOUND WITH A KNIFE STUCK IN YOUR AMPLE, BLUBBERY BACK BEFORE THEN!

THEY'LL HAVE TO GO THROUGH YOU FIRST, BLUTCH! FROM NOW ON, YOU'LL SLEEP IN MY ROOM, ACROSS THE DOORWAY!

WHAT?!

114.

THERE ARE NO REGULATIONS FORCING ME TO SHARE THE ROOM OF A SUPERIOR! I REFUSE!

I DO!

YOU DO?

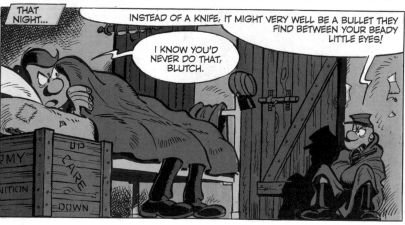

THAT NIGHT...

INSTEAD OF A KNIFE, IT MIGHT VERY WELL BE A BULLET THEY FIND BETWEEN YOUR BEADY LITTLE EYES!

I KNOW YOU'D NEVER DO THAT, BLUTCH.

OH YEAH?... AND WHAT MAKES YOU THINK SO, HUH?

I KNOW THAT, DEEP DOWN, YOU LIKE ME!

WHAT?
I...

KLIK

ISN'T THAT RIGHT, BLUTCH?...

WELL... YEAH... A BIT, I GUESS... HA HA HA...

GOOD NIGHT, CORPORAL.

GOOD NIGHT, SERGEANT!

MB

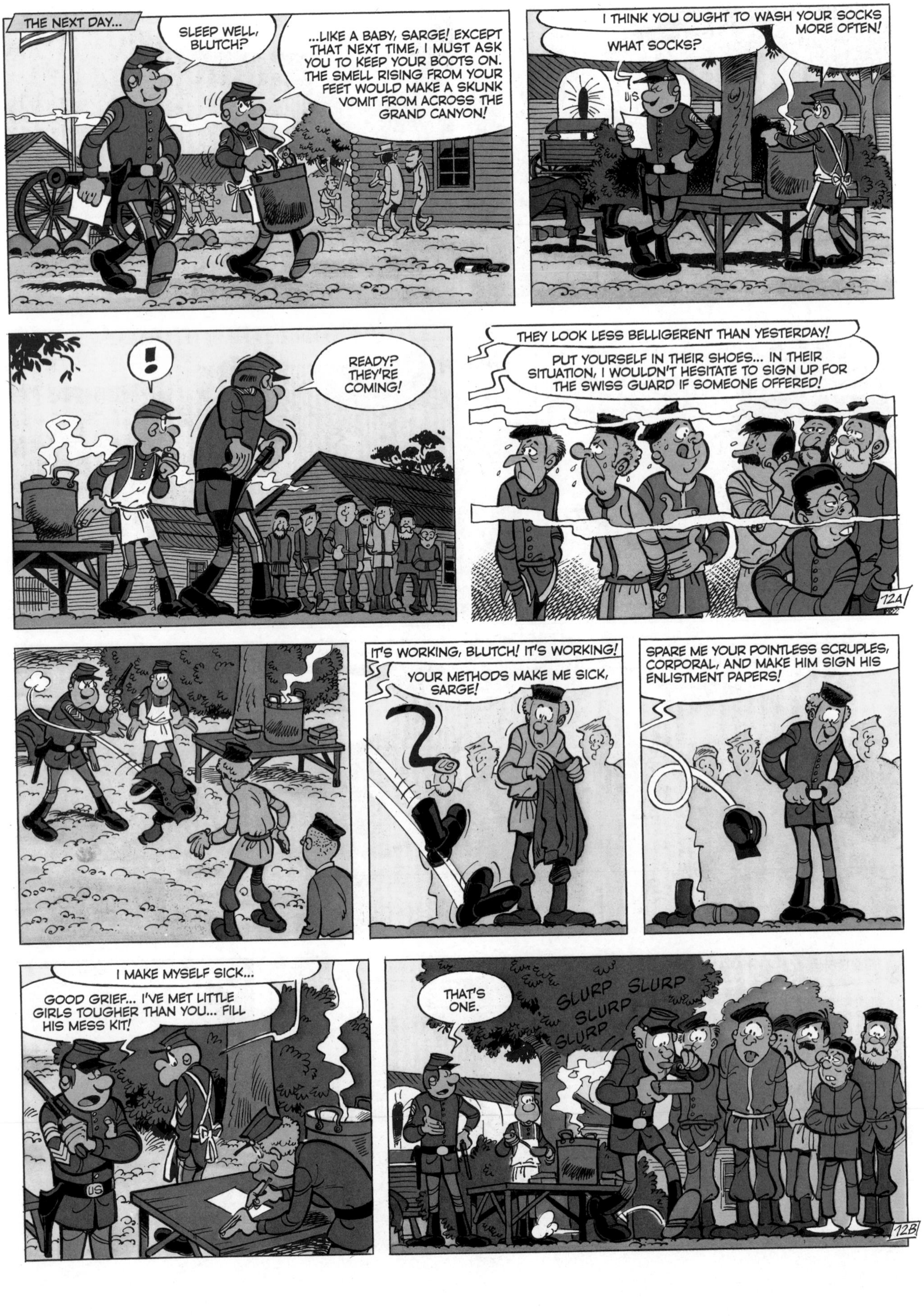
THE NEXT DAY...
SLEEP WELL, BLUTCH?
...LIKE A BABY, SARGE! EXCEPT THAT NEXT TIME, I MUST ASK YOU TO KEEP YOUR BOOTS ON. THE SMELL RISING FROM YOUR FEET WOULD MAKE A SKUNK VOMIT FROM ACROSS THE GRAND CANYON!
I THINK YOU OUGHT TO WASH YOUR SOCKS MORE OFTEN!
WHAT SOCKS?
!
READY? THEY'RE COMING!
THEY LOOK LESS BELLIGERENT THAN YESTERDAY!
PUT YOURSELF IN THEIR SHOES... IN THEIR SITUATION, I WOULDN'T HESITATE TO SIGN UP FOR THE SWISS GUARD IF SOMEONE OFFERED!
12A
IT'S WORKING, BLUTCH! IT'S WORKING!
YOUR METHODS MAKE ME SICK, SARGE!
SPARE ME YOUR POINTLESS SCRUPLES, CORPORAL, AND MAKE HIM SIGN HIS ENLISTMENT PAPERS!
I MAKE MYSELF SICK...
GOOD GRIEF... I'VE MET LITTLE GIRLS TOUGHER THAN YOU... FILL HIS MESS KIT!
THAT'S ONE.
SLURP SLURP SLURP SLURP
12B

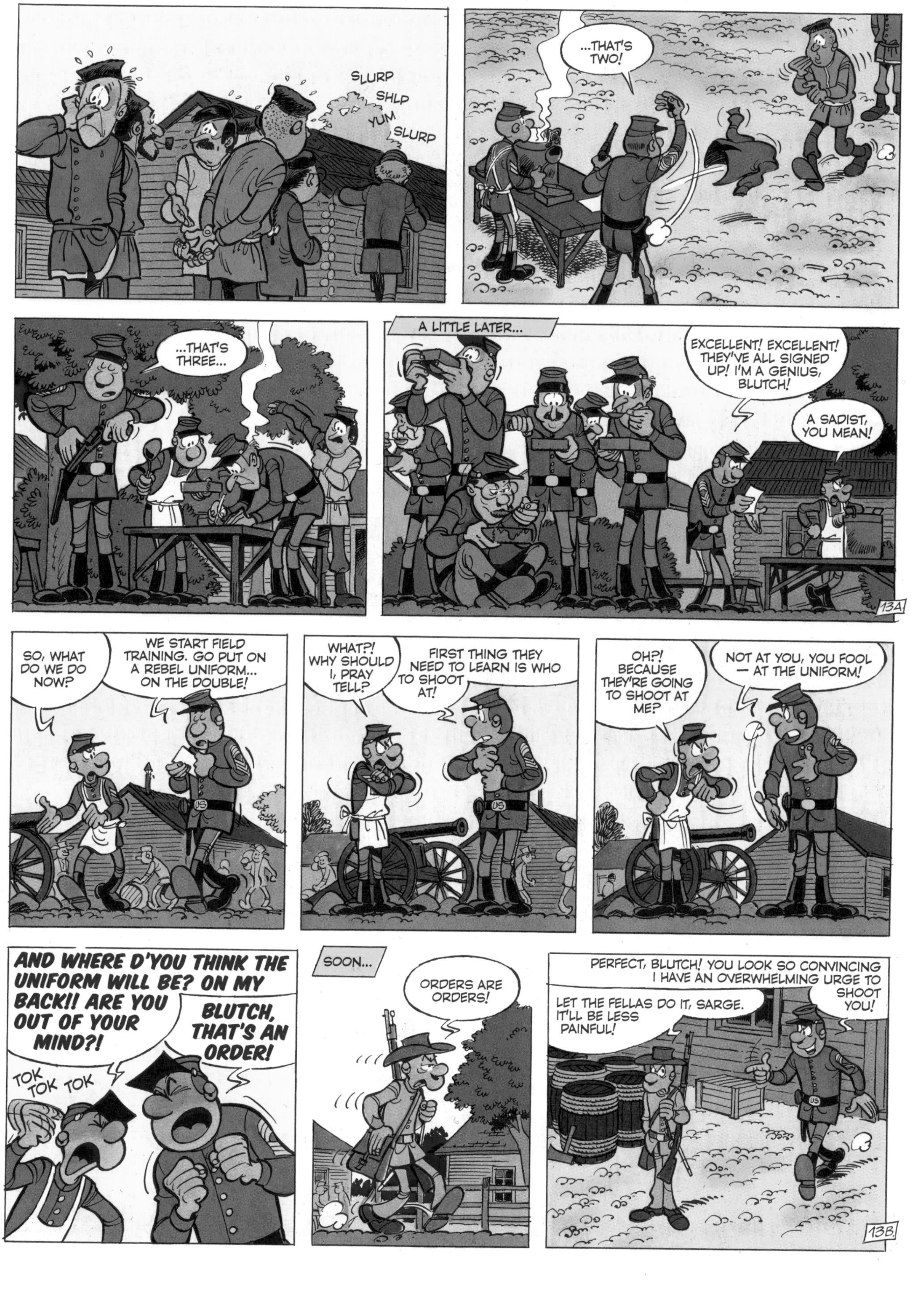
SLURP
SHLP
YUM
SLURP
...THAT'S TWO!
...THAT'S THREE...
A LITTLE LATER...
EXCELLENT! EXCELLENT! THEY'VE ALL SIGNED UP! I'M A GENIUS, BLUTCH!
A SADIST, YOU MEAN!
13A
SO, WHAT DO WE DO NOW?
WE START FIELD TRAINING. GO PUT ON A REBEL UNIFORM... ON THE DOUBLE!
WHAT?! WHY SHOULD I, PRAY TELL?
FIRST THING THEY NEED TO LEARN IS WHO TO SHOOT AT!
OH?! BECAUSE THEY'RE GOING TO SHOOT AT ME?
NOT AT YOU, YOU FOOL — AT THE UNIFORM!
AND WHERE D'YOU THINK THE UNIFORM WILL BE? ON MY BACK!! ARE YOU OUT OF YOUR MIND?!
BLUTCH, THAT'S AN ORDER!
TOK TOK TOK
SOON...
ORDERS ARE ORDERS!
PERFECT, BLUTCH! YOU LOOK SO CONVINCING I HAVE AN OVERWHELMING URGE TO SHOOT YOU!
LET THE FELLAS DO IT, SARGE. IT'LL BE LESS PAINFUL!
13B

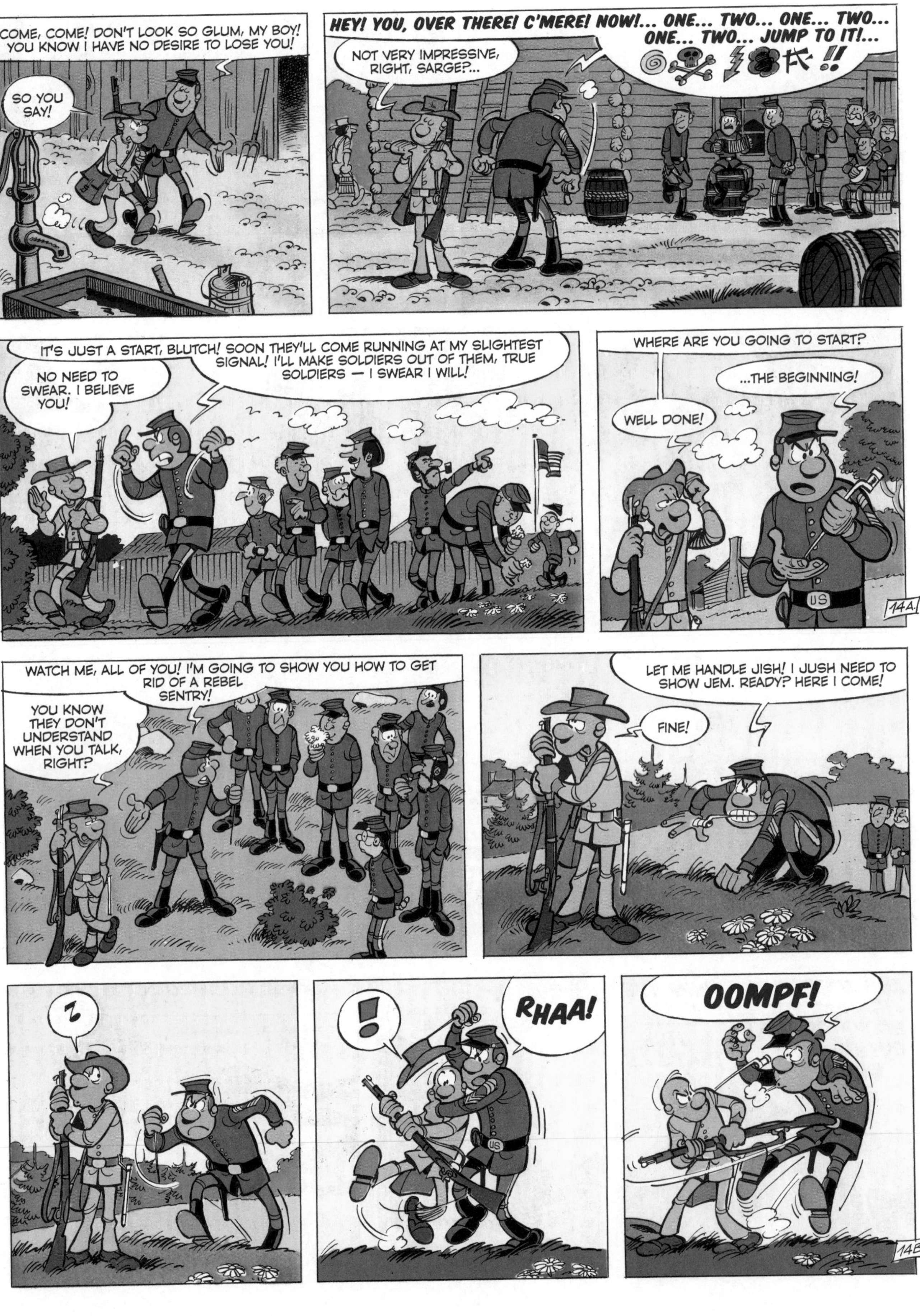
COME, COME! DON'T LOOK SO GLUM, MY BOY! YOU KNOW I HAVE NO DESIRE TO LOSE YOU!
SO YOU SAY!
HEY! YOU, OVER THERE! C'MERE! NOW!... ONE... TWO... ONE... TWO... ONE... TWO... JUMP TO IT!...
NOT VERY IMPRESSIVE, RIGHT, SARGE?...
IT'S JUST A START, BLUTCH! SOON THEY'LL COME RUNNING AT MY SLIGHTEST SIGNAL! I'LL MAKE SOLDIERS OUT OF THEM, TRUE SOLDIERS — I SWEAR I WILL!
NO NEED TO SWEAR. I BELIEVE YOU!
WHERE ARE YOU GOING TO START?
...THE BEGINNING!
WELL DONE!
US
14A.
WATCH ME, ALL OF YOU! I'M GOING TO SHOW YOU HOW TO GET RID OF A REBEL SENTRY!
YOU KNOW THEY DON'T UNDERSTAND WHEN YOU TALK, RIGHT?
LET ME HANDLE JISH! I JUSH NEED TO SHOW JEM. READY? HERE I COME!
FINE!
?
!
RHAA!
US
OOMPF!
14B.

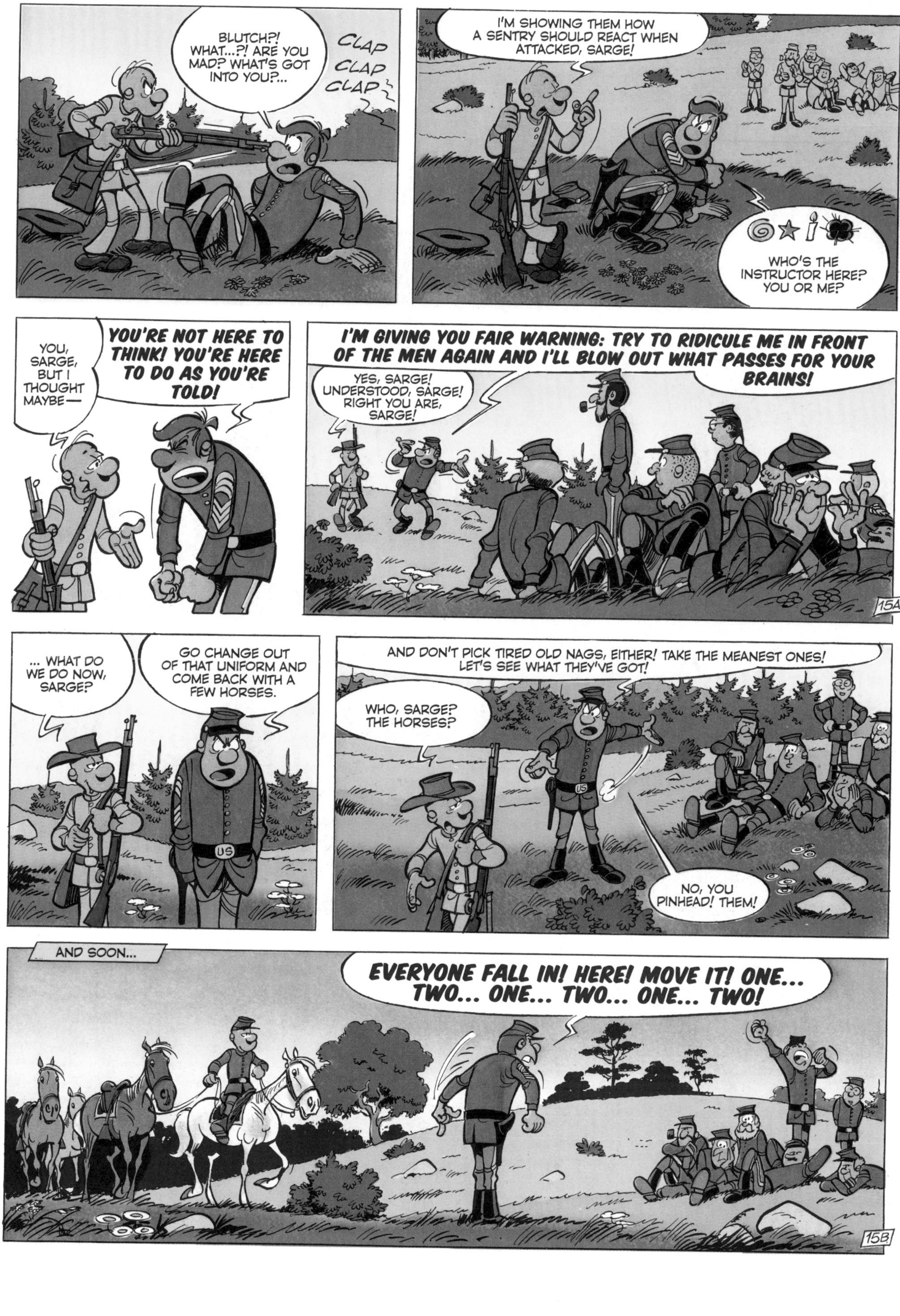

BLUTCH?! WHAT...?! ARE YOU MAD? WHAT'S GOT INTO YOU?...
CLAP CLAP CLAP
I'M SHOWING THEM HOW A SENTRY SHOULD REACT WHEN ATTACKED, SARGE!
WHO'S THE INSTRUCTOR HERE? YOU OR ME?
YOU, SARGE, BUT I THOUGHT MAYBE—
YOU'RE NOT HERE TO THINK! YOU'RE HERE TO DO AS YOU'RE TOLD!
I'M GIVING YOU FAIR WARNING: TRY TO RIDICULE ME IN FRONT OF THE MEN AGAIN AND I'LL BLOW OUT WHAT PASSES FOR YOUR BRAINS!
YES, SARGE! UNDERSTOOD, SARGE! RIGHT YOU ARE, SARGE!
15A.
... WHAT DO WE DO NOW, SARGE?
GO CHANGE OUT OF THAT UNIFORM AND COME BACK WITH A FEW HORSES.
AND DON'T PICK TIRED OLD NAGS, EITHER! TAKE THE MEANEST ONES! LET'S SEE WHAT THEY'VE GOT!
WHO, SARGE? THE HORSES?
NO, YOU PINHEAD! THEM!
AND SOON...
EVERYONE FALL IN! HERE! MOVE IT! ONE... TWO... ONE... TWO... ONE... TWO!
15B

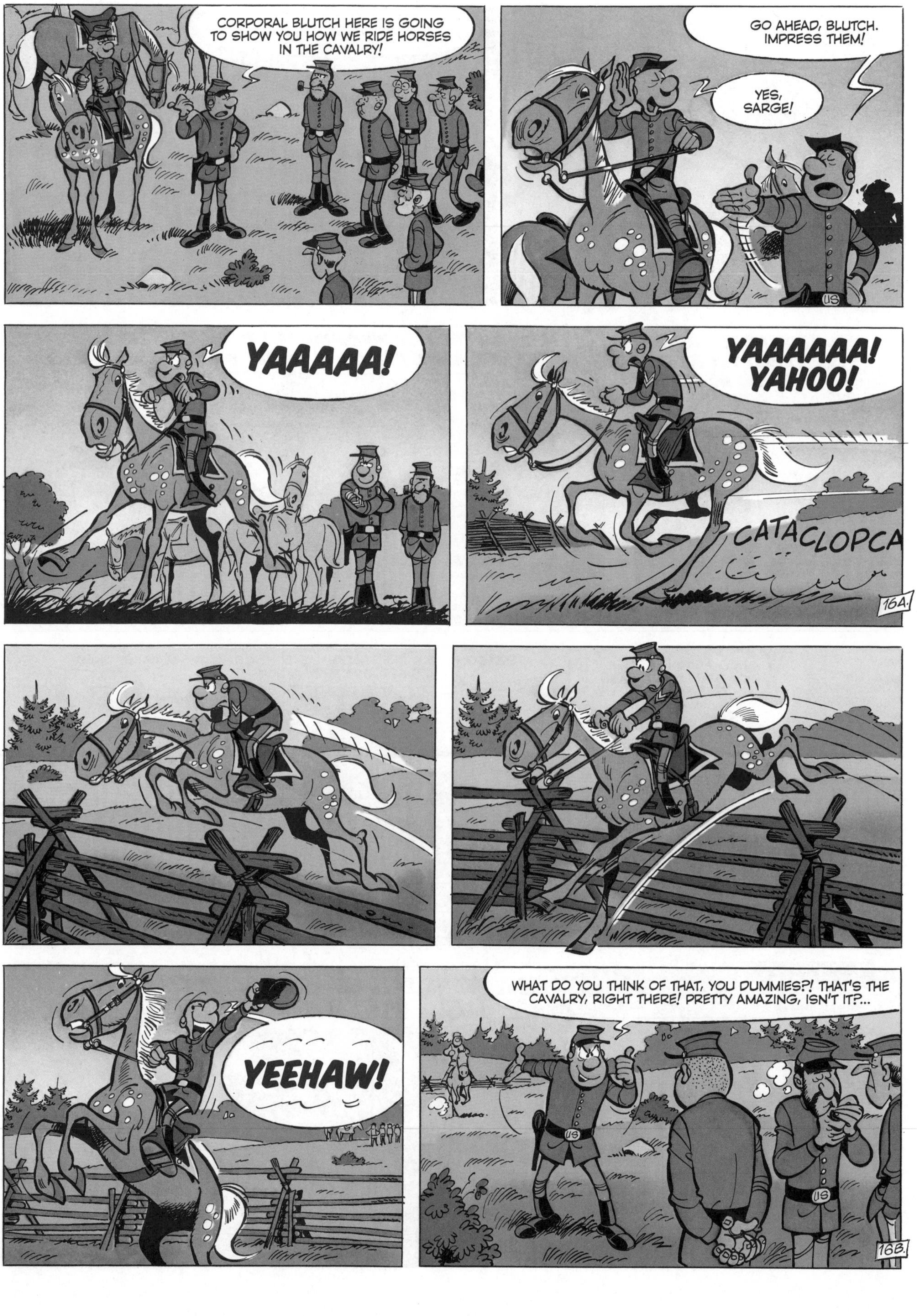

CORPORAL BLUTCH HERE IS GOING TO SHOW YOU HOW WE RIDE HORSES IN THE CAVALRY!
GO AHEAD, BLUTCH. IMPRESS THEM!
YES, SARGE!
YAAAAA!
YAAAAAA! YAHOO!
CATACLOPCA
16A.
YEEHAW!
WHAT DO YOU THINK OF THAT, YOU DUMMIES?! THAT'S THE CAVALRY, RIGHT THERE! PRETTY AMAZING, ISN'T IT?...
16B.

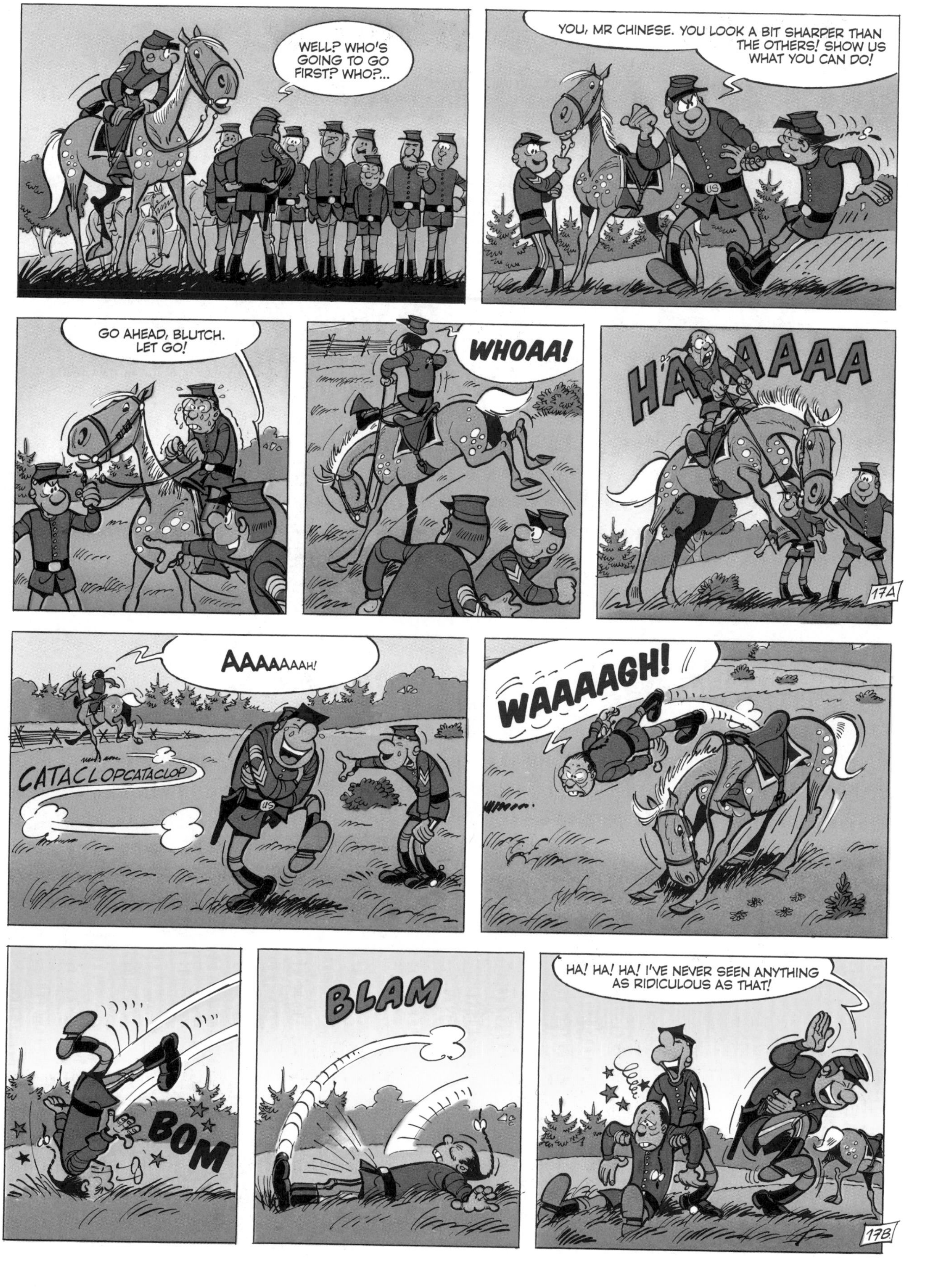
WELL? WHO'S GOING TO GO FIRST? WHO?...
YOU, MR CHINESE. YOU LOOK A BIT SHARPER THAN THE OTHERS! SHOW US WHAT YOU CAN DO!
GO AHEAD, BLUTCH. LET GO!
WHOAA!
HAAAAAA
17A
AAAAAAAH!
CATACLOPCATACLOP
WAAAAGH!
BOM
BLAM
HA! HA! HA! I'VE NEVER SEEN ANYTHING AS RIDICULOUS AS THAT!
17B

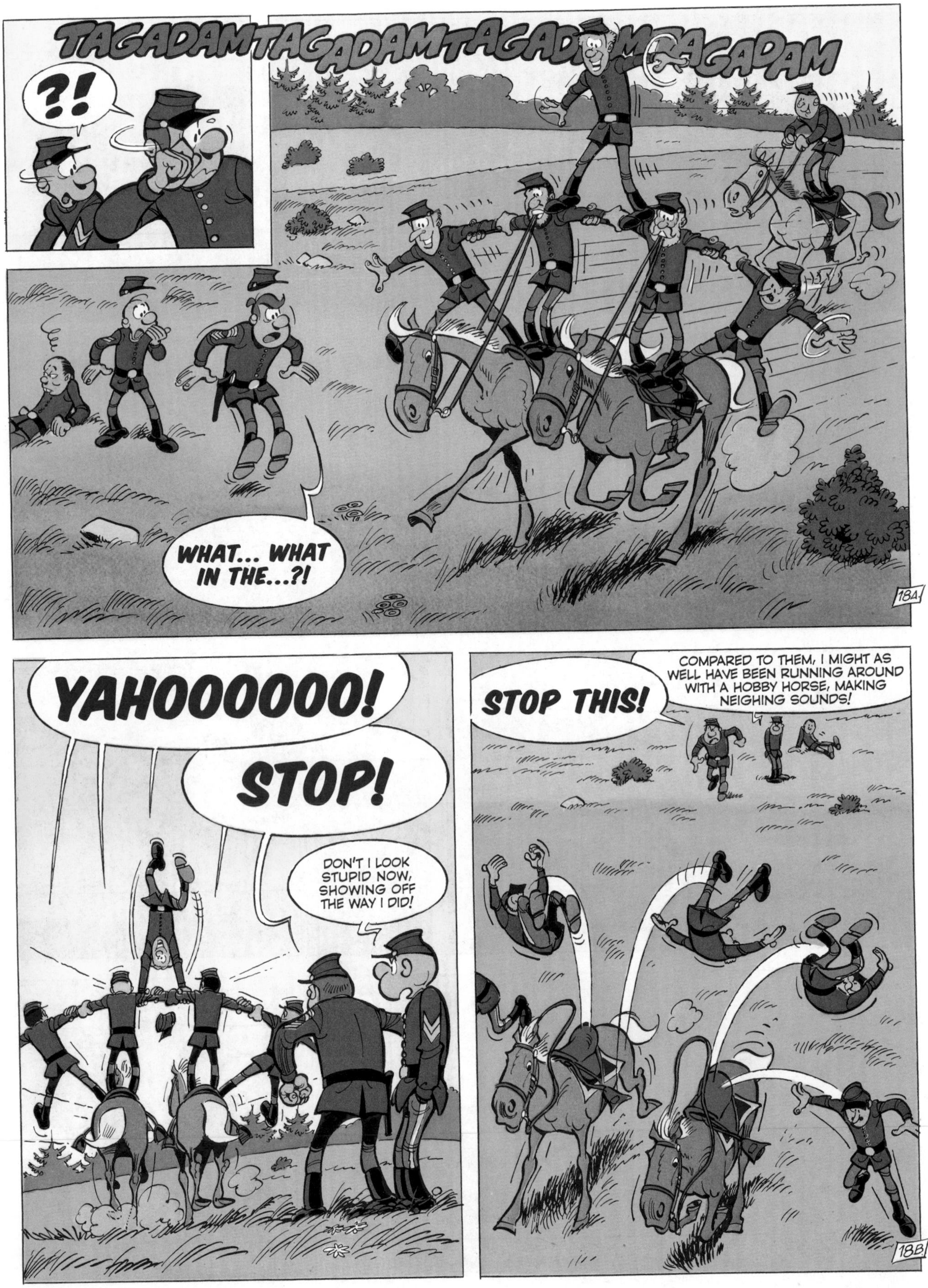

?!
TAGADAMTAGADAMTAGAD
AGADAM
WHAT... WHAT IN THE...?!
18A
YAHOOOOOOO!
STOP!
DON'T I LOOK STUPID NOW, SHOWING OFF THE WAY I DID!
STOP THIS!
COMPARED TO THEM, I MIGHT AS WELL HAVE BEEN RUNNING AROUND WITH A HOBBY HORSE, MAKING NEIGHING SOUNDS!
18B

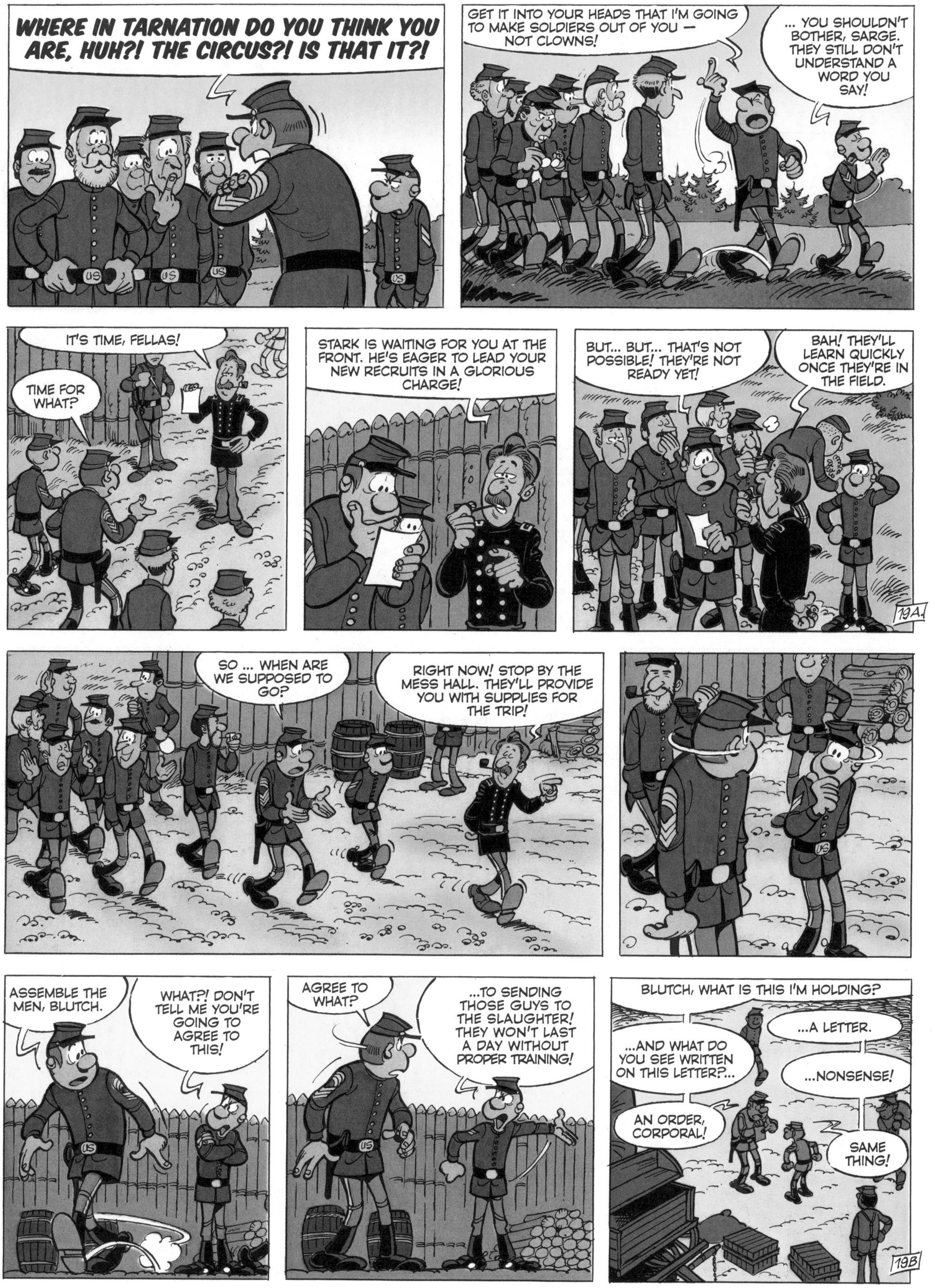
WHERE IN TARNATION DO YOU THINK YOU ARE, HUH?! THE CIRCUS?! IS THAT IT?!
GET IT INTO YOUR HEADS THAT I'M GOING TO MAKE SOLDIERS OUT OF YOU — NOT CLOWNS!
... YOU SHOULDN'T BOTHER, SARGE. THEY STILL DON'T UNDERSTAND A WORD YOU SAY!
IT'S TIME, FELLAS!
TIME FOR WHAT?
STARK IS WAITING FOR YOU AT THE FRONT. HE'S EAGER TO LEAD YOUR NEW RECRUITS IN A GLORIOUS CHARGE!
BUT... BUT... THAT'S NOT POSSIBLE! THEY'RE NOT READY YET!
BAH! THEY'LL LEARN QUICKLY ONCE THEY'RE IN THE FIELD.
19A.
SO ... WHEN ARE WE SUPPOSED TO GO?
RIGHT NOW! STOP BY THE MESS HALL. THEY'LL PROVIDE YOU WITH SUPPLIES FOR THE TRIP!
ASSEMBLE THE MEN, BLUTCH.
WHAT?! DON'T TELL ME YOU'RE GOING TO AGREE TO THIS!
AGREE TO WHAT?
...TO SENDING THOSE GUYS TO THE SLAUGHTER! THEY WON'T LAST A DAY WITHOUT PROPER TRAINING!
BLUTCH, WHAT IS THIS I'M HOLDING?
...A LETTER.
...AND WHAT DO YOU SEE WRITTEN ON THIS LETTER?...
...NONSENSE!
AN ORDER, CORPORAL!
SAME THING!
19B

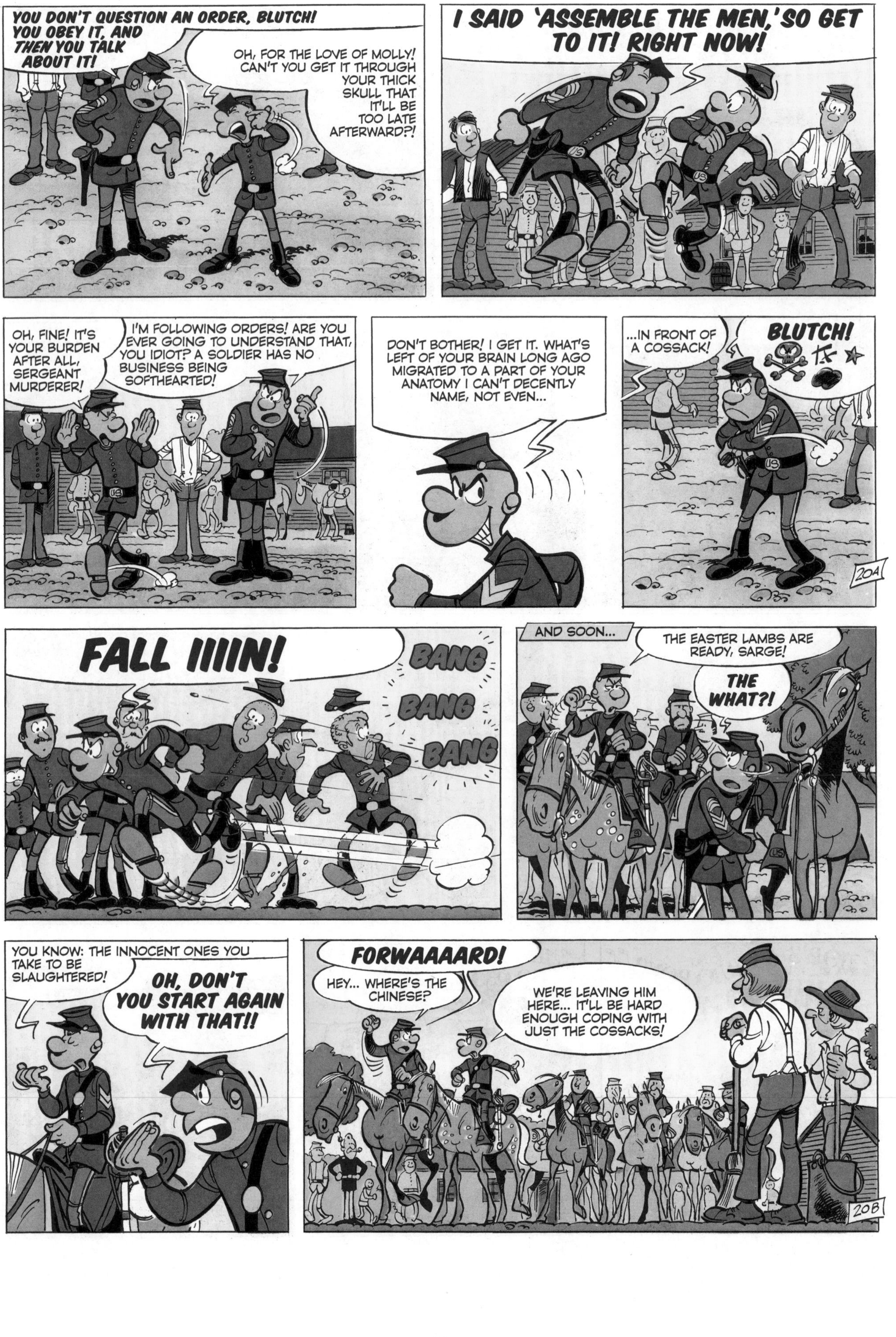
YOU DON'T QUESTION AN ORDER, BLUTCH! YOU OBEY IT, AND THEN YOU TALK ABOUT IT!
OH, FOR THE LOVE OF MOLLY! CAN'T YOU GET IT THROUGH YOUR THICK SKULL THAT IT'LL BE TOO LATE AFTERWARD?!
I SAID 'ASSEMBLE THE MEN,' SO GET TO IT! RIGHT NOW!
OH, FINE! IT'S YOUR BURDEN AFTER ALL, SERGEANT MURDERER!
I'M FOLLOWING ORDERS! ARE YOU EVER GOING TO UNDERSTAND THAT, YOU IDIOT? A SOLDIER HAS NO BUSINESS BEING SOFTHEARTED!
DON'T BOTHER! I GET IT. WHAT'S LEFT OF YOUR BRAIN LONG AGO MIGRATED TO A PART OF YOUR ANATOMY I CAN'T DECENTLY NAME, NOT EVEN...
...IN FRONT OF A COSSACK!
BLUTCH!
20A
FALL IIIIN!
BANG
BANG
BANG
AND SOON...
THE EASTER LAMBS ARE READY, SARGE!
THE WHAT?!
YOU KNOW: THE INNOCENT ONES YOU TAKE TO BE SLAUGHTERED!
OH, DON'T YOU START AGAIN WITH THAT!!
FORWAAAARD!
HEY... WHERE'S THE CHINESE?
WE'RE LEAVING HIM HERE... IT'LL BE HARD ENOUGH COPING WITH JUST THE COSSACKS!
20B

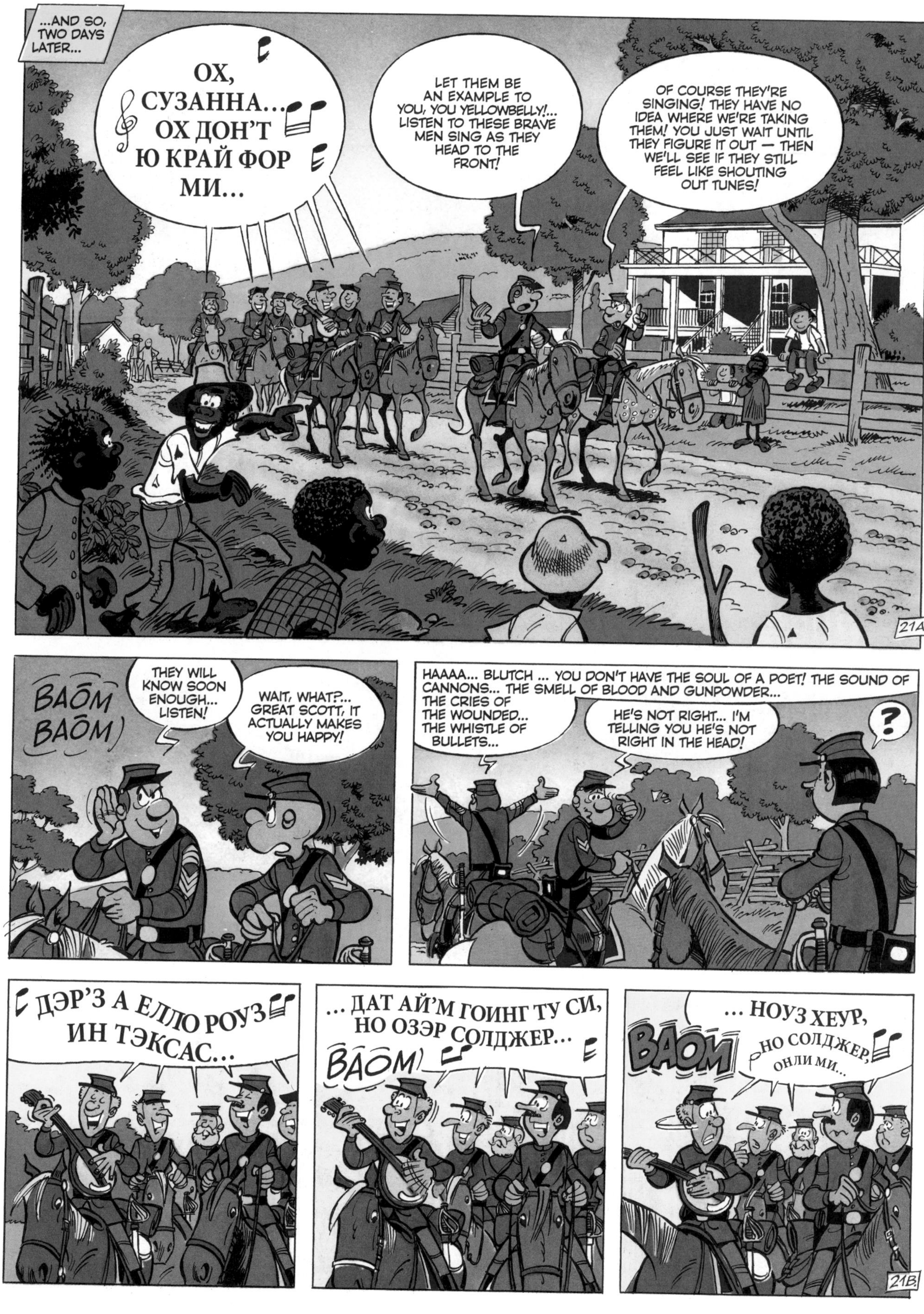

...AND SO, TWO DAYS LATER...
ОХ, СУЗАННА... ОХ ДОН'Т Ю КРАЙ ФОР МИ...
LET THEM BE AN EXAMPLE TO YOU, YOU YELLOWBELLY!... LISTEN TO THESE BRAVE MEN SING AS THEY HEAD TO THE FRONT!
OF COURSE THEY'RE SINGING! THEY HAVE NO IDEA WHERE WE'RE TAKING THEM! YOU JUST WAIT UNTIL THEY FIGURE IT OUT — THEN WE'LL SEE IF THEY STILL FEEL LIKE SHOUTING OUT TUNES!
21A.
BAOM BAOM
THEY WILL KNOW SOON ENOUGH... LISTEN!
WAIT, WHAT?... GREAT SCOTT, IT ACTUALLY MAKES YOU HAPPY!
HAAAA... BLUTCH ... YOU DON'T HAVE THE SOUL OF A POET! THE SOUND OF CANNONS... THE SMELL OF BLOOD AND GUNPOWDER... THE CRIES OF THE WOUNDED... THE WHISTLE OF BULLETS...
HE'S NOT RIGHT... I'M TELLING YOU HE'S NOT RIGHT IN THE HEAD!
?
ДЭР'З А ЕЛЛО РОУЗ ИН ТЭКСАС...
... ДАТ АЙ'М ГОИНГ ТУ СИ, НО ОЗЭР СОЛДЖЕР...
BAOM
... НОУЗ ХЕУР,
BAOM
НО СОЛДЖЕР, ОНЛИ МИ...
21B.

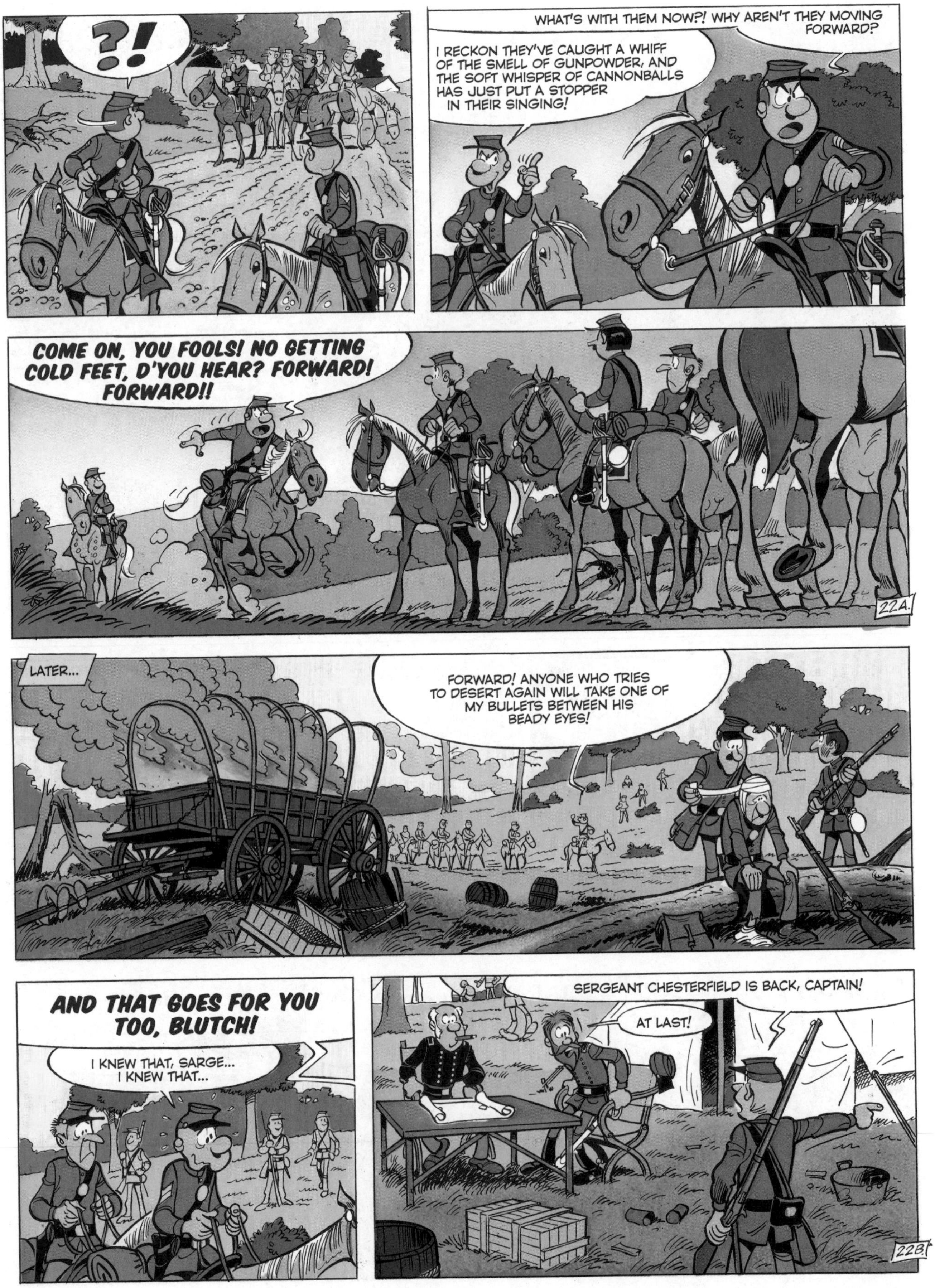
?!
WHAT'S WITH THEM NOW?! WHY AREN'T THEY MOVING FORWARD?
I RECKON THEY'VE CAUGHT A WHIFF OF THE SMELL OF GUNPOWDER, AND THE SOFT WHISPER OF CANNONBALLS HAS JUST PUT A STOPPER IN THEIR SINGING!
COME ON, YOU FOOLS! NO GETTING COLD FEET, D'YOU HEAR? FORWARD! FORWARD!!
22A.
LATER...
FORWARD! ANYONE WHO TRIES TO DESERT AGAIN WILL TAKE ONE OF MY BULLETS BETWEEN HIS BEADY EYES!
AND THAT GOES FOR YOU TOO, BLUTCH!
I KNEW THAT, SARGE... I KNEW THAT...
SERGEANT CHESTERFIELD IS BACK, CAPTAIN!
AT LAST!
22B.

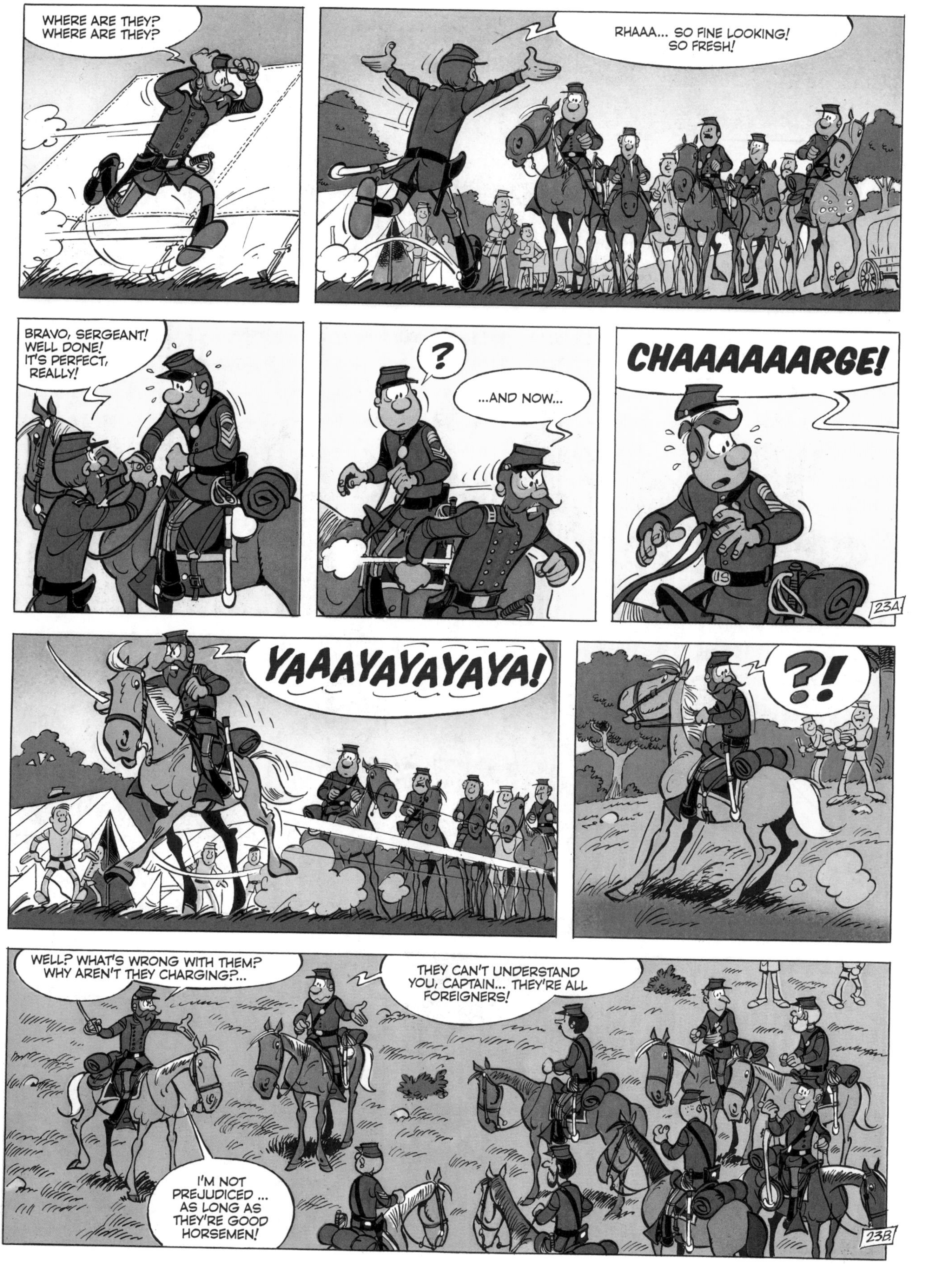
WHERE ARE THEY? WHERE ARE THEY?
RHAAA... SO FINE LOOKING! SO FRESH!
BRAVO, SERGEANT! WELL DONE! IT'S PERFECT, REALLY!
?
...AND NOW...
CHAAAAAAARGE!
23A
YAAAYAYAYAYA!
?!
WELL? WHAT'S WRONG WITH THEM? WHY AREN'T THEY CHARGING?...
THEY CAN'T UNDERSTAND YOU, CAPTAIN... THEY'RE ALL FOREIGNERS!
I'M NOT PREJUDICED ... AS LONG AS THEY'RE GOOD HORSEMEN!
23B

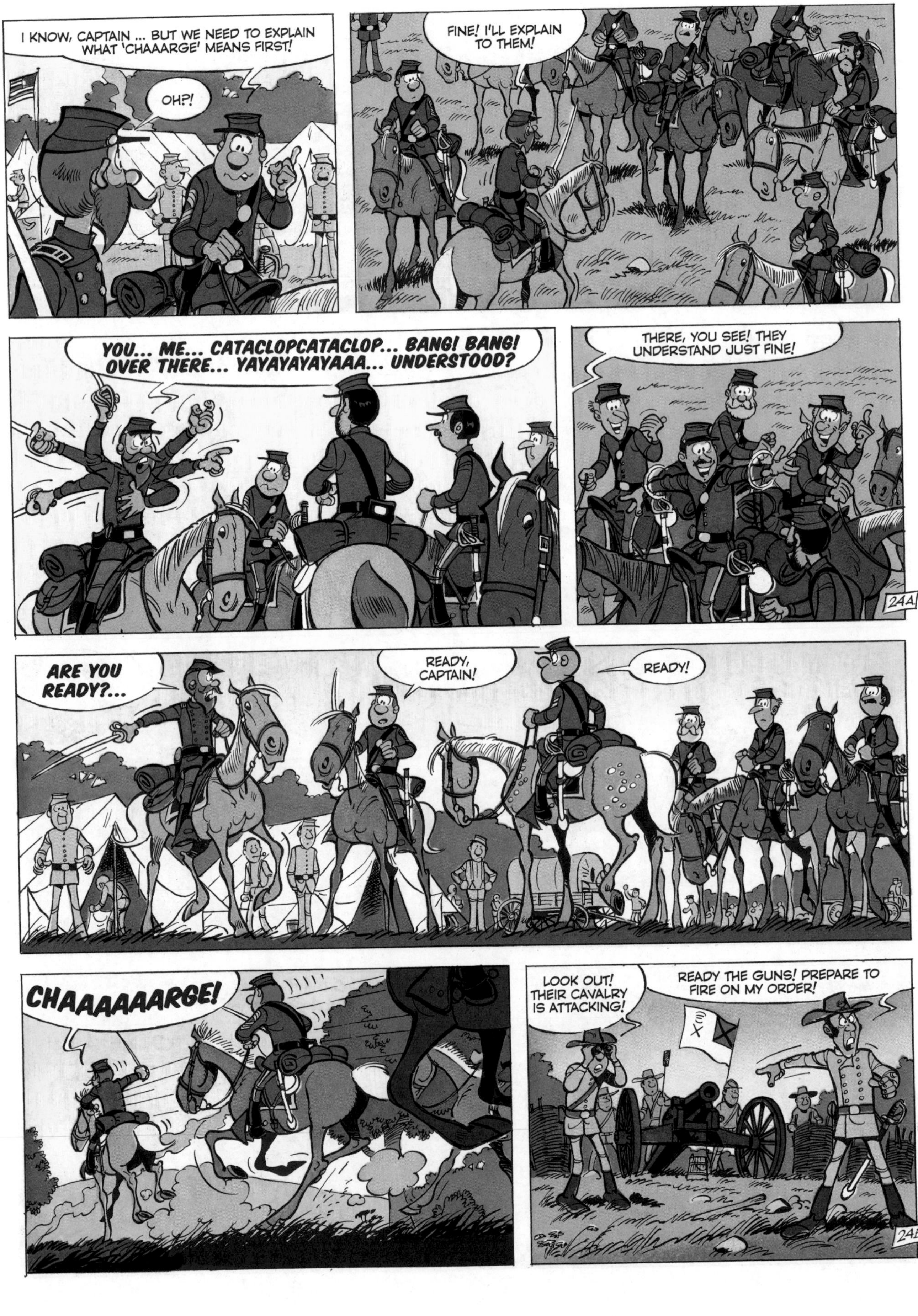
I KNOW, CAPTAIN ... BUT WE NEED TO EXPLAIN WHAT 'CHAAARGE' MEANS FIRST!
OH?!
FINE! I'LL EXPLAIN TO THEM!
YOU... ME... CATACLOPCATACLOP... BANG! BANG! OVER THERE... YAYAYAYAYAAA... UNDERSTOOD?
THERE, YOU SEE! THEY UNDERSTAND JUST FINE!
24A
ARE YOU READY?...
READY, CAPTAIN!
READY!
CHAAAAAARGE!
LOOK OUT! THEIR CAVALRY IS ATTACKING!
READY THE GUNS! PREPARE TO FIRE ON MY ORDER!
24B

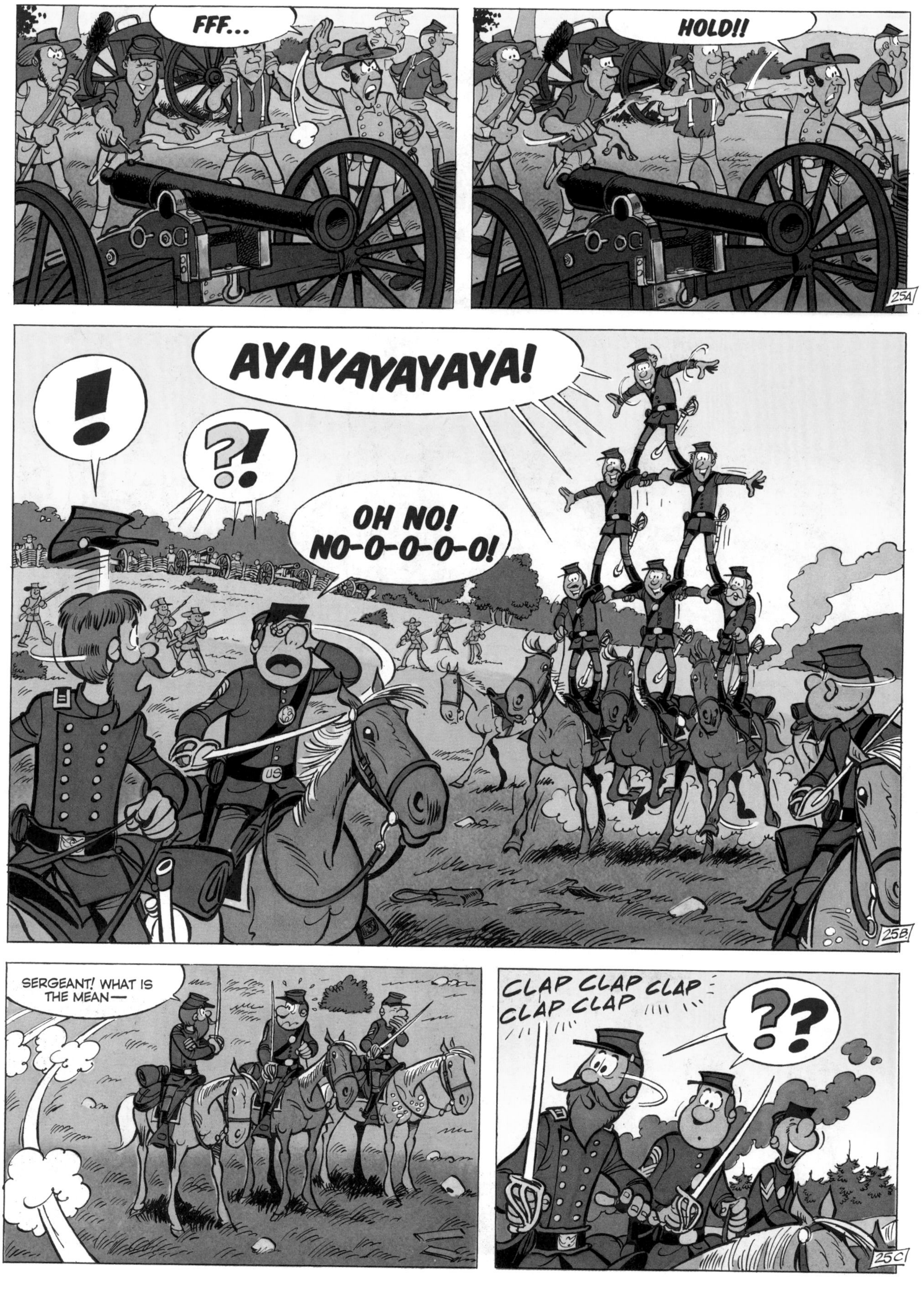
FFF...
HOLD!!
AYAYAYAYAYAYA!
!
?!
OH NO!
NO-O-O-O-O!
SERGEANT! WHAT IS THE MEAN—
CLAP CLAP CLAP
CLAP CLAP
??

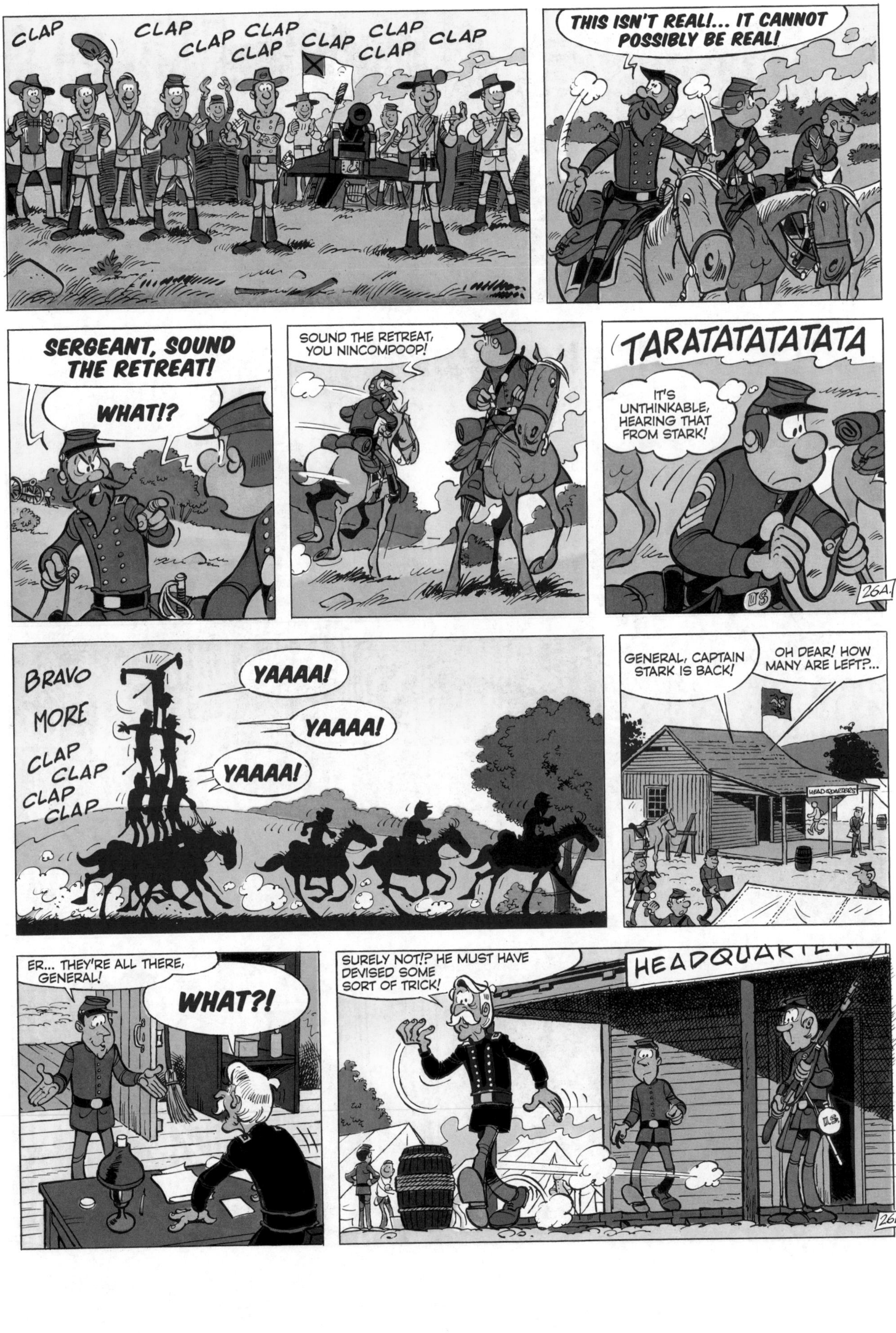
CLAP CLAP CLAP CLAP CLAP CLAP CLAP CLAP CLAP
THIS ISN'T REAL!... IT CANNOT POSSIBLY BE REAL!
SERGEANT, SOUND THE RETREAT!
WHAT!?
SOUND THE RETREAT, YOU NINCOMPOOP!
TARATATATATATA
IT'S UNTHINKABLE, HEARING THAT FROM STARK!
26A
BRAVO
MORE
CLAP CLAP CLAP CLAP
YAAAA!
YAAAA!
YAAAA!
GENERAL, CAPTAIN STARK IS BACK!
OH DEAR! HOW MANY ARE LEFT?...
ER... THEY'RE ALL THERE, GENERAL!
WHAT?!
SURELY NOT!? HE MUST HAVE DEVISED SOME SORT OF TRICK!
HEADQUARTER
26B

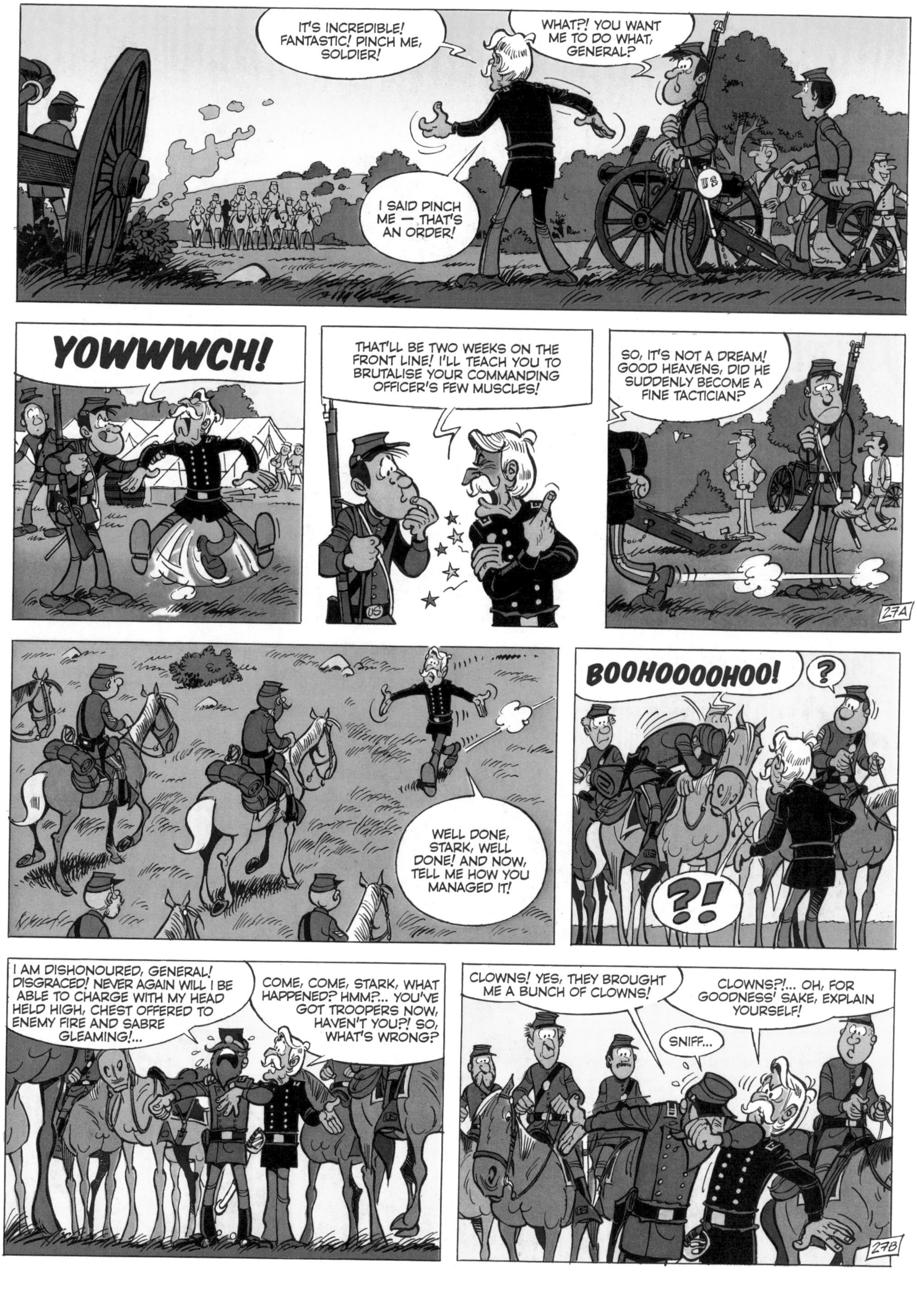
IT'S INCREDIBLE! FANTASTIC! PINCH ME, SOLDIER!
WHAT?! YOU WANT ME TO DO WHAT, GENERAL?
I SAID PINCH ME — THAT'S AN ORDER!
YOWWWCH!
THAT'LL BE TWO WEEKS ON THE FRONT LINE! I'LL TEACH YOU TO BRUTALISE YOUR COMMANDING OFFICER'S FEW MUSCLES!
SO, IT'S NOT A DREAM! GOOD HEAVENS, DID HE SUDDENLY BECOME A FINE TACTICIAN?
27A
WELL DONE, STARK, WELL DONE! AND NOW, TELL ME HOW YOU MANAGED IT!
BOOHOOOOHOO!
?
?!
I AM DISHONOURED, GENERAL! DISGRACED! NEVER AGAIN WILL I BE ABLE TO CHARGE WITH MY HEAD HELD HIGH, CHEST OFFERED TO ENEMY FIRE AND SABRE GLEAMING!...
COME, COME, STARK, WHAT HAPPENED? HMM?... YOU'VE GOT TROOPERS NOW, HAVEN'T YOU?! SO, WHAT'S WRONG?
CLOWNS! YES, THEY BROUGHT ME A BUNCH OF CLOWNS!
CLOWNS?!... OH, FOR GOODNESS' SAKE, EXPLAIN YOURSELF!
SNIFF...
27B

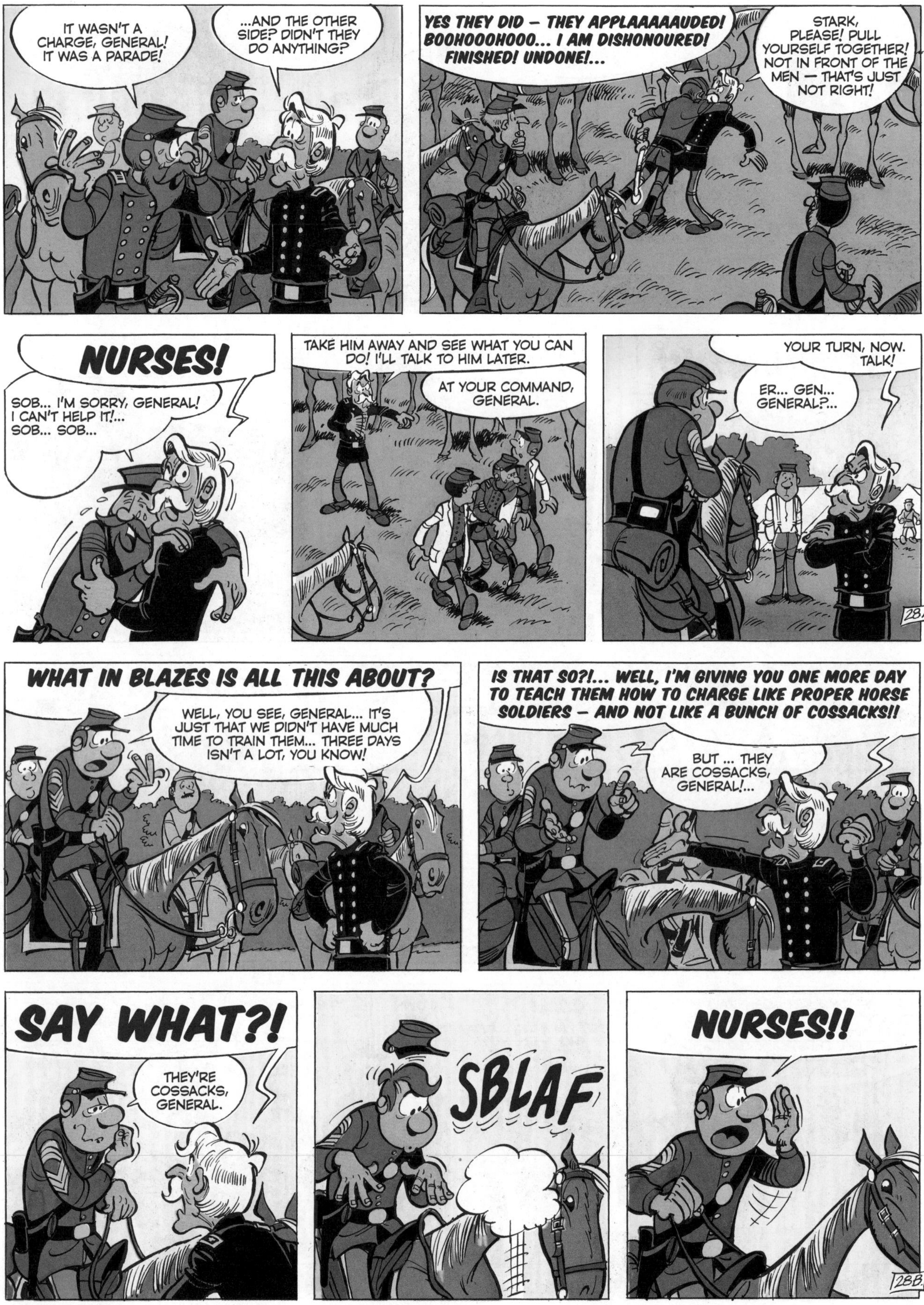
IT WASN'T A CHARGE, GENERAL! IT WAS A PARADE!
...AND THE OTHER SIDE? DIDN'T THEY DO ANYTHING?
YES THEY DID – THEY APPLAAAAAUDED! BOOHOOOHOOO... I AM DISHONOURED! FINISHED! UNDONE!...
STARK, PLEASE! PULL YOURSELF TOGETHER! NOT IN FRONT OF THE MEN — THAT'S JUST NOT RIGHT!
NURSES!
SOB... I'M SORRY, GENERAL! I CAN'T HELP IT!... SOB... SOB...
TAKE HIM AWAY AND SEE WHAT YOU CAN DO! I'LL TALK TO HIM LATER.
AT YOUR COMMAND, GENERAL.
YOUR TURN, NOW. TALK!
ER... GEN... GENERAL?...
28A
WHAT IN BLAZES IS ALL THIS ABOUT?
WELL, YOU SEE, GENERAL... IT'S JUST THAT WE DIDN'T HAVE MUCH TIME TO TRAIN THEM... THREE DAYS ISN'T A LOT, YOU KNOW!
IS THAT SO?!... WELL, I'M GIVING YOU ONE MORE DAY TO TEACH THEM HOW TO CHARGE LIKE PROPER HORSE SOLDIERS – AND NOT LIKE A BUNCH OF COSSACKS!!
BUT ... THEY ARE COSSACKS, GENERAL!...
SAY WHAT?!
THEY'RE COSSACKS, GENERAL.
SBLAF
NURSES!!
28B.

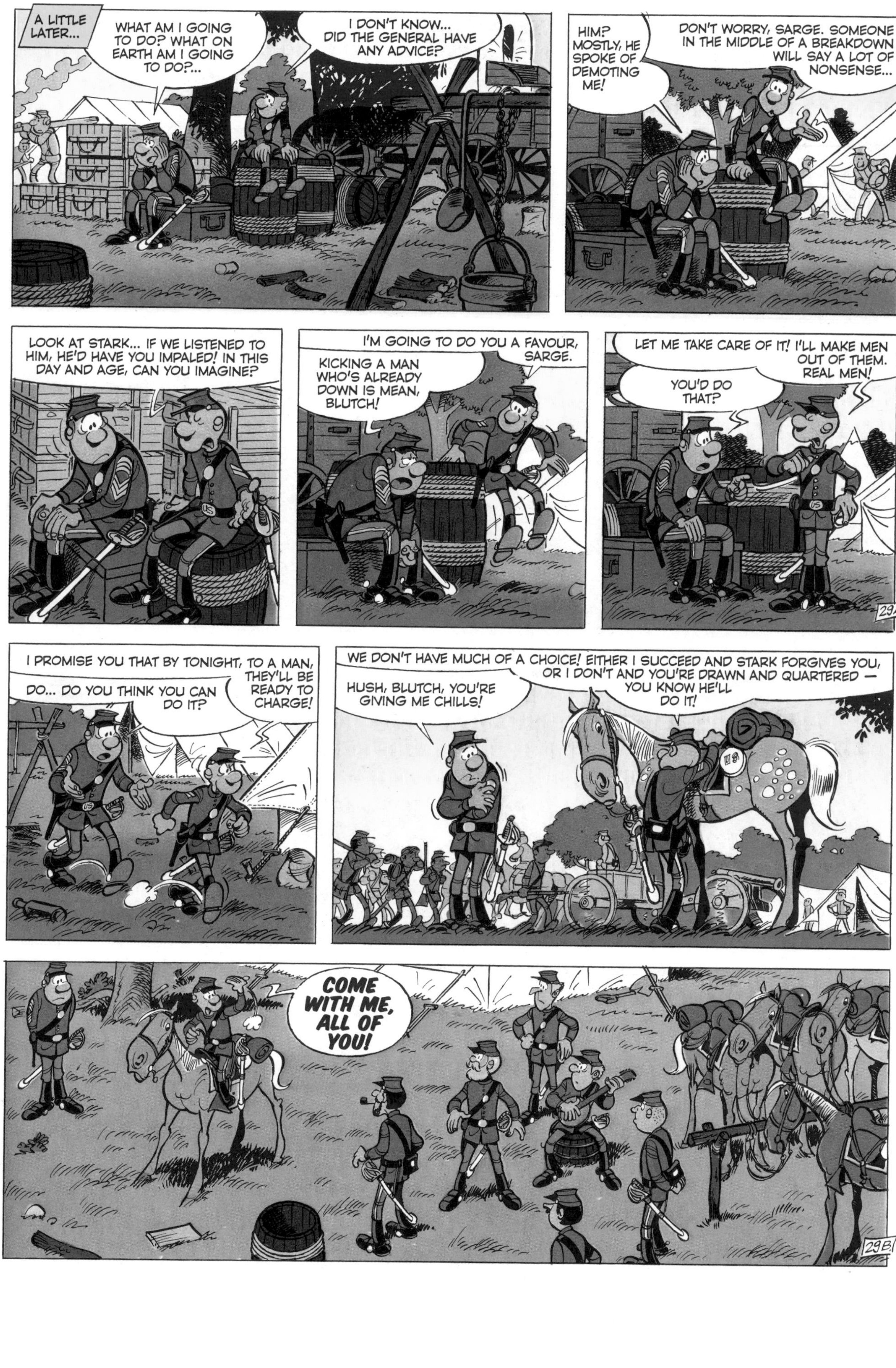
A LITTLE LATER...
WHAT AM I GOING TO DO? WHAT ON EARTH AM I GOING TO DO?...
I DON'T KNOW... DID THE GENERAL HAVE ANY ADVICE?
HIM? MOSTLY, HE SPOKE OF DEMOTING ME!
DON'T WORRY, SARGE. SOMEONE IN THE MIDDLE OF A BREAKDOWN WILL SAY A LOT OF NONSENSE...
LOOK AT STARK... IF WE LISTENED TO HIM, HE'D HAVE YOU IMPALED! IN THIS DAY AND AGE, CAN YOU IMAGINE?
KICKING A MAN WHO'S ALREADY DOWN IS MEAN, BLUTCH!
I'M GOING TO DO YOU A FAVOUR, SARGE.
LET ME TAKE CARE OF IT! I'LL MAKE MEN OUT OF THEM. REAL MEN!
YOU'D DO THAT?
29A.
I PROMISE YOU THAT BY TONIGHT, TO A MAN, THEY'LL BE READY TO CHARGE!
DO... DO YOU THINK YOU CAN DO IT?
WE DON'T HAVE MUCH OF A CHOICE! EITHER I SUCCEED AND STARK FORGIVES YOU, OR I DON'T AND YOU'RE DRAWN AND QUARTERED — YOU KNOW HE'LL DO IT!
HUSH, BLUTCH, YOU'RE GIVING ME CHILLS!
COME WITH ME, ALL OF YOU!
29B.

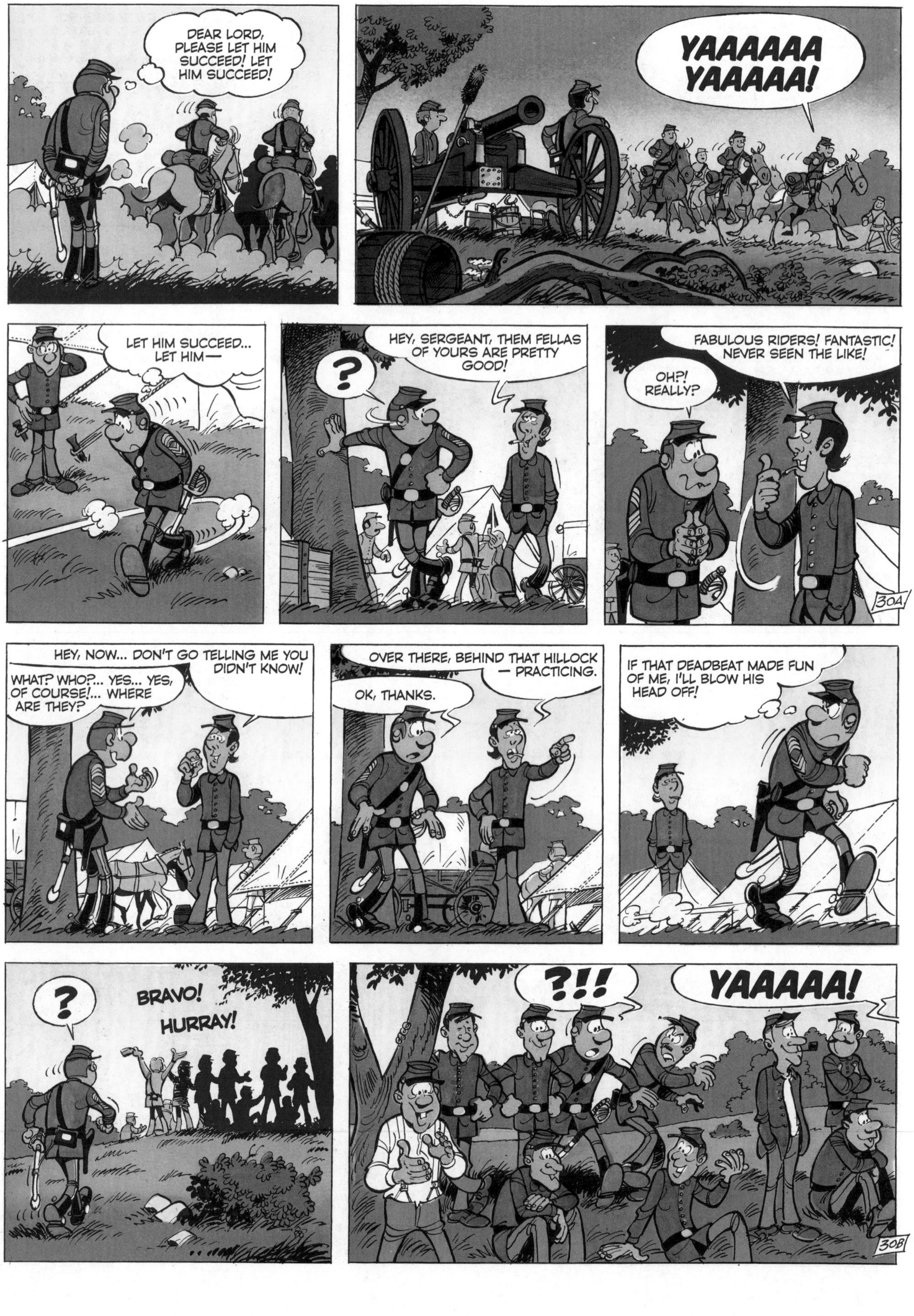
DEAR LORD, PLEASE LET HIM SUCCEED! LET HIM SUCCEED!
YAAAAAA YAAAAA!
LET HIM SUCCEED... LET HIM—
HEY, SERGEANT, THEM FELLAS OF YOURS ARE PRETTY GOOD!
?
FABULOUS RIDERS! FANTASTIC! NEVER SEEN THE LIKE!
OH?! REALLY?
30A
HEY, NOW... DON'T GO TELLING ME YOU DIDN'T KNOW!
WHAT? WHO?... YES... YES, OF COURSE!... WHERE ARE THEY?
OVER THERE, BEHIND THAT HILLOCK — PRACTICING.
OK, THANKS.
IF THAT DEADBEAT MADE FUN OF ME, I'LL BLOW HIS HEAD OFF!
?
BRAVO!
HURRAY!
?!!
YAAAAA!
30B

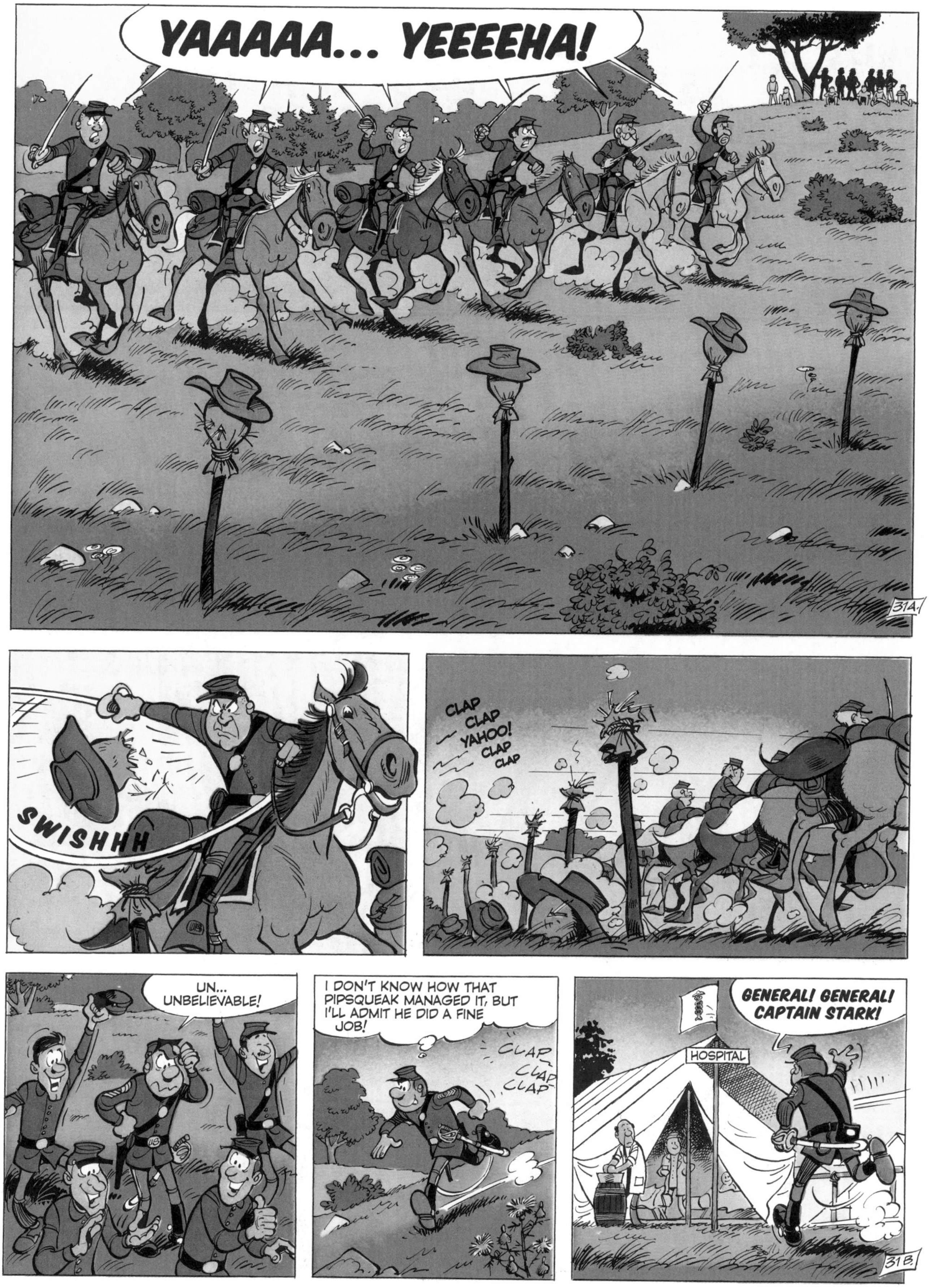
YAAAAA... YEEEEHA!
31A.
SWISHHH
CLAP
CLAP
YAHOO!
CLAP
CLAP
UN... UNBELIEVABLE!
I DON'T KNOW HOW THAT PIPSQUEAK MANAGED IT, BUT I'LL ADMIT HE DID A FINE JOB!
CLAP
CLAP
CLAP
HOSPITAL
GENERAL! GENERAL! CAPTAIN STARK!
31B.

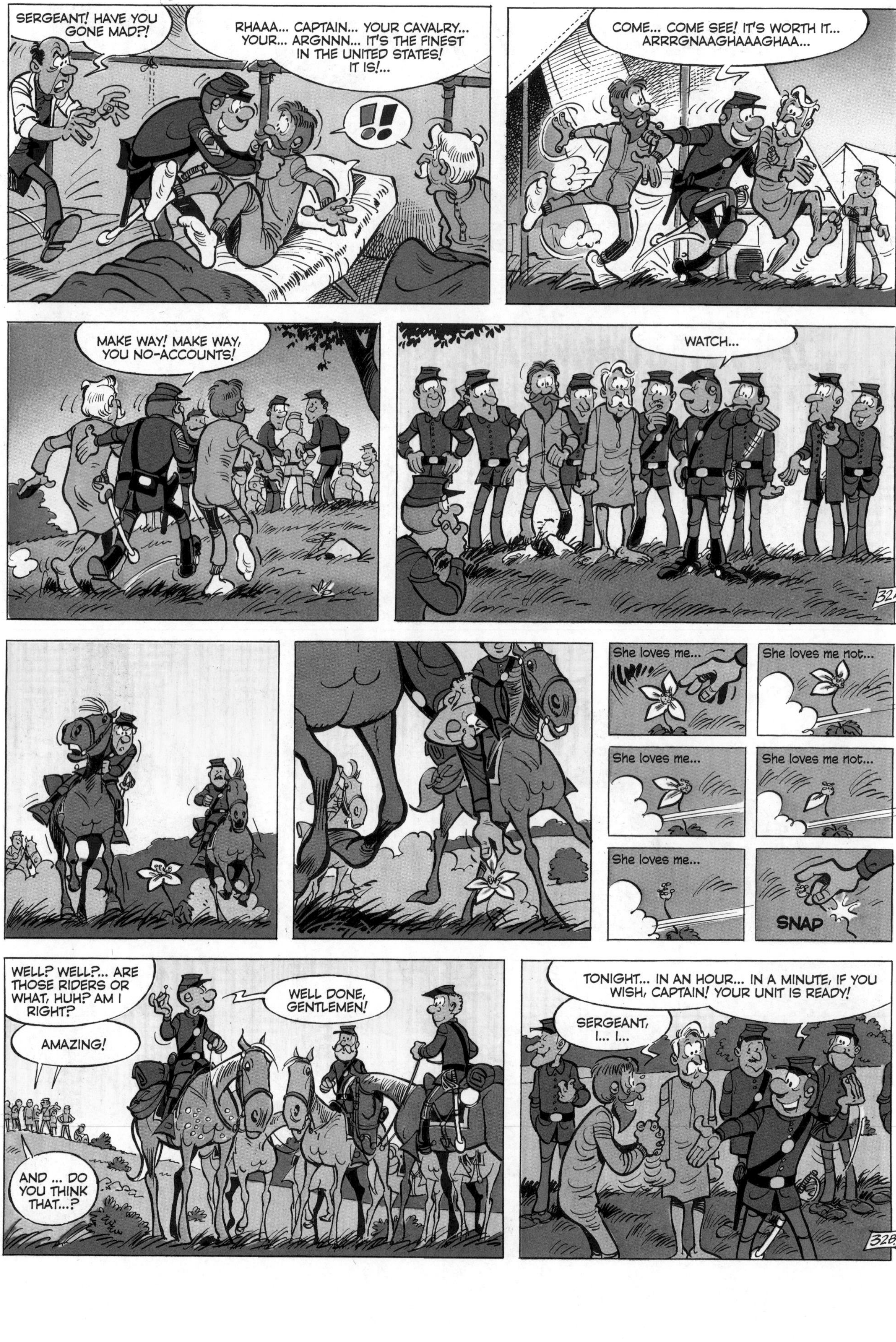

SERGEANT! HAVE YOU GONE MAD?!
RHAAA... CAPTAIN... YOUR CAVALRY... YOUR... ARGNNN... IT'S THE FINEST IN THE UNITED STATES! IT IS!...
!!
COME... COME SEE! IT'S WORTH IT... ARRRGNAAGHAAAGHAA...
MAKE WAY! MAKE WAY, YOU NO-ACCOUNTS!
WATCH...
32A
She loves me...
She loves me not...
She loves me...
She loves me not...
She loves me...
SNAP
WELL? WELL?... ARE THOSE RIDERS OR WHAT, HUH? AM I RIGHT?
WELL DONE, GENTLEMEN!
AMAZING!
AND ... DO YOU THINK THAT...?
TONIGHT... IN AN HOUR... IN A MINUTE, IF YOU WISH, CAPTAIN! YOUR UNIT IS READY!
SERGEANT, I... I...
32B

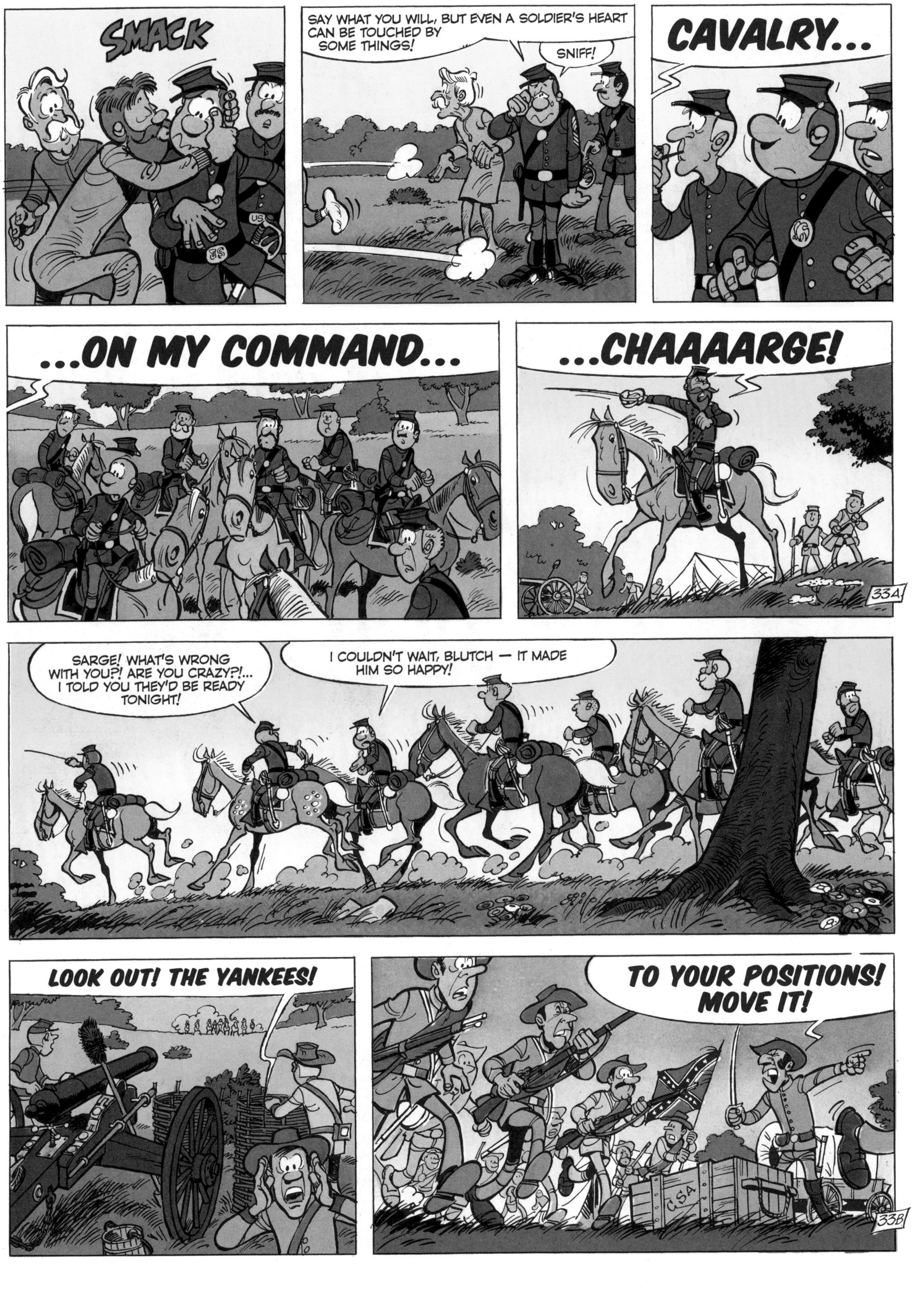
SMACK
SAY WHAT YOU WILL, BUT EVEN A SOLDIER'S HEART CAN BE TOUCHED BY SOME THINGS!
SNIFF!
CAVALRY...
...ON MY COMMAND...
...CHAAAARGE!
33A
SARGE! WHAT'S WRONG WITH YOU?! ARE YOU CRAZY?!... I TOLD YOU THEY'D BE READY TONIGHT!
I COULDN'T WAIT, BLUTCH — IT MADE HIM SO HAPPY!
LOOK OUT! THE YANKEES!
TO YOUR POSITIONS! MOVE IT!
33B

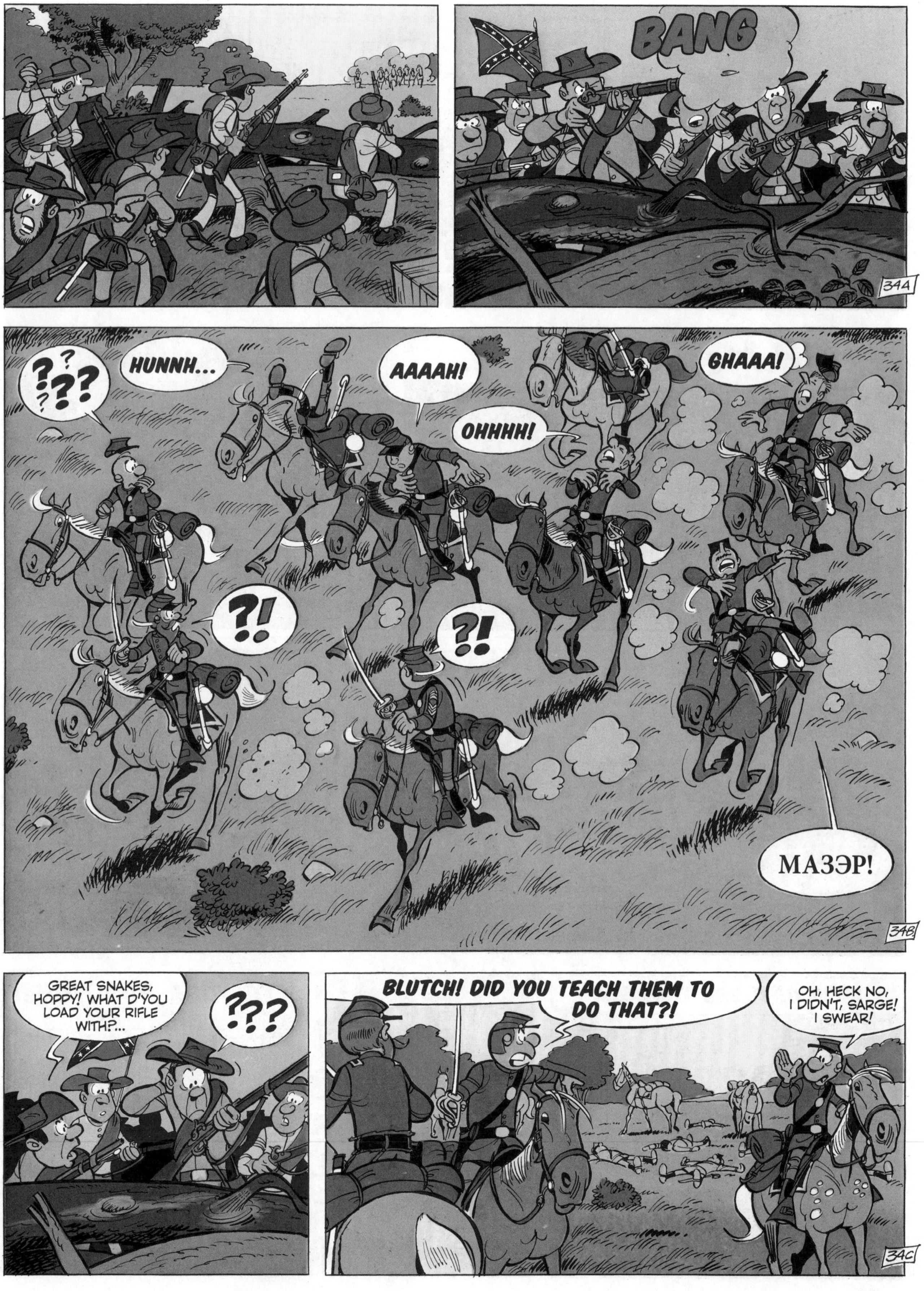
BANG
34A
???
HUNNH...
AAAAH!
OHHHH!
GHAAA!
?!
?!
МАЗЭР!
34B
GREAT SNAKES, HOPPY! WHAT D'YOU LOAD YOUR RIFLE WITH?...
???
BLUTCH! DID YOU TEACH THEM TO DO THAT?!
OH, HECK NO, I DIDN'T, SARGE! I SWEAR!
34C

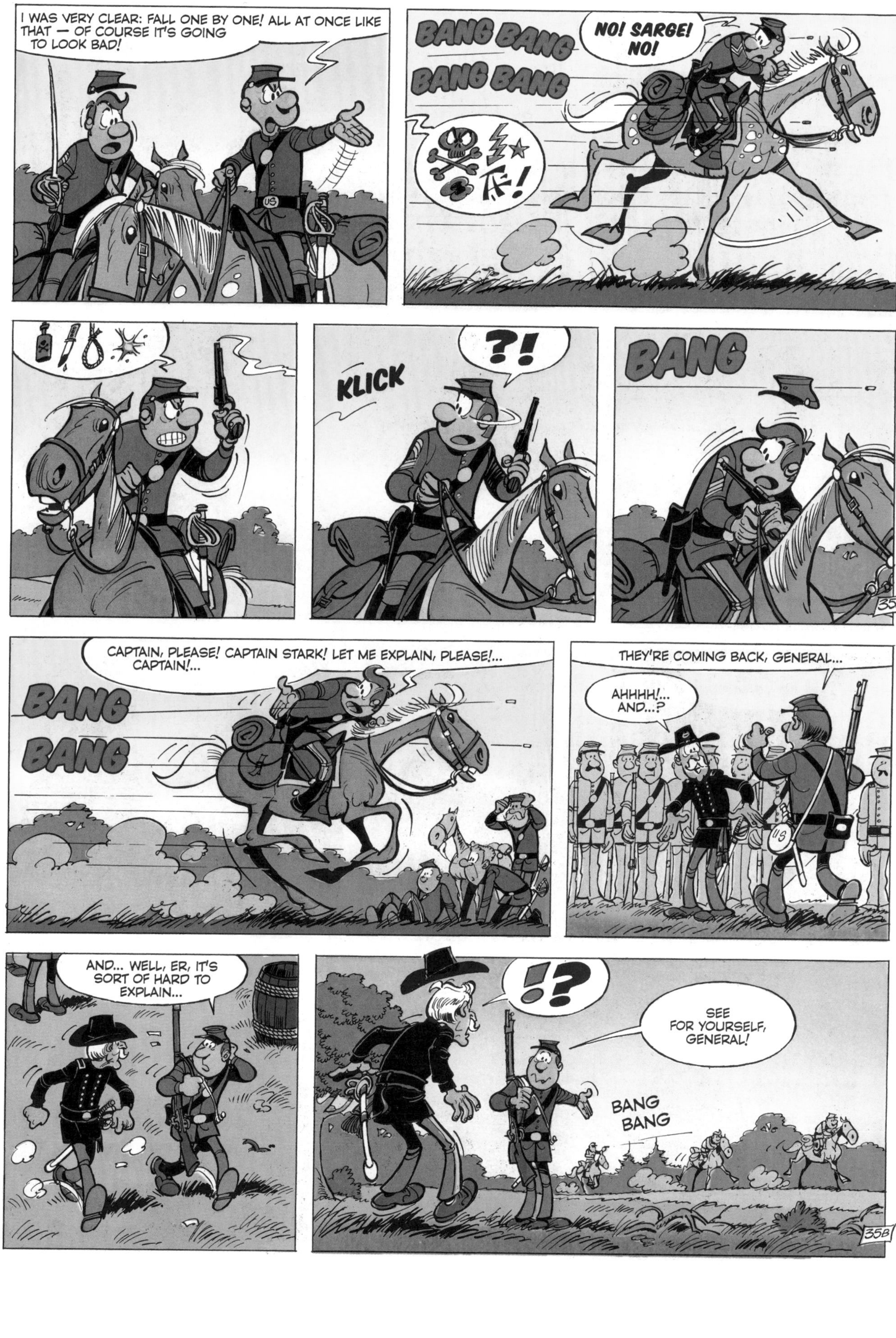

I WAS VERY CLEAR: FALL ONE BY ONE! ALL AT ONCE LIKE THAT — OF COURSE IT'S GOING TO LOOK BAD!
BANG BANG
BANG BANG
NO! SARGE! NO!
KLICK
?!
BANG
35A
CAPTAIN, PLEASE! CAPTAIN STARK! LET ME EXPLAIN, PLEASE!... CAPTAIN!...
BANG
BANG
THEY'RE COMING BACK, GENERAL...
AHHHH!... AND...?
AND... WELL, ER, IT'S SORT OF HARD TO EXPLAIN...
!?
SEE FOR YOURSELF, GENERAL!
BANG BANG
35B

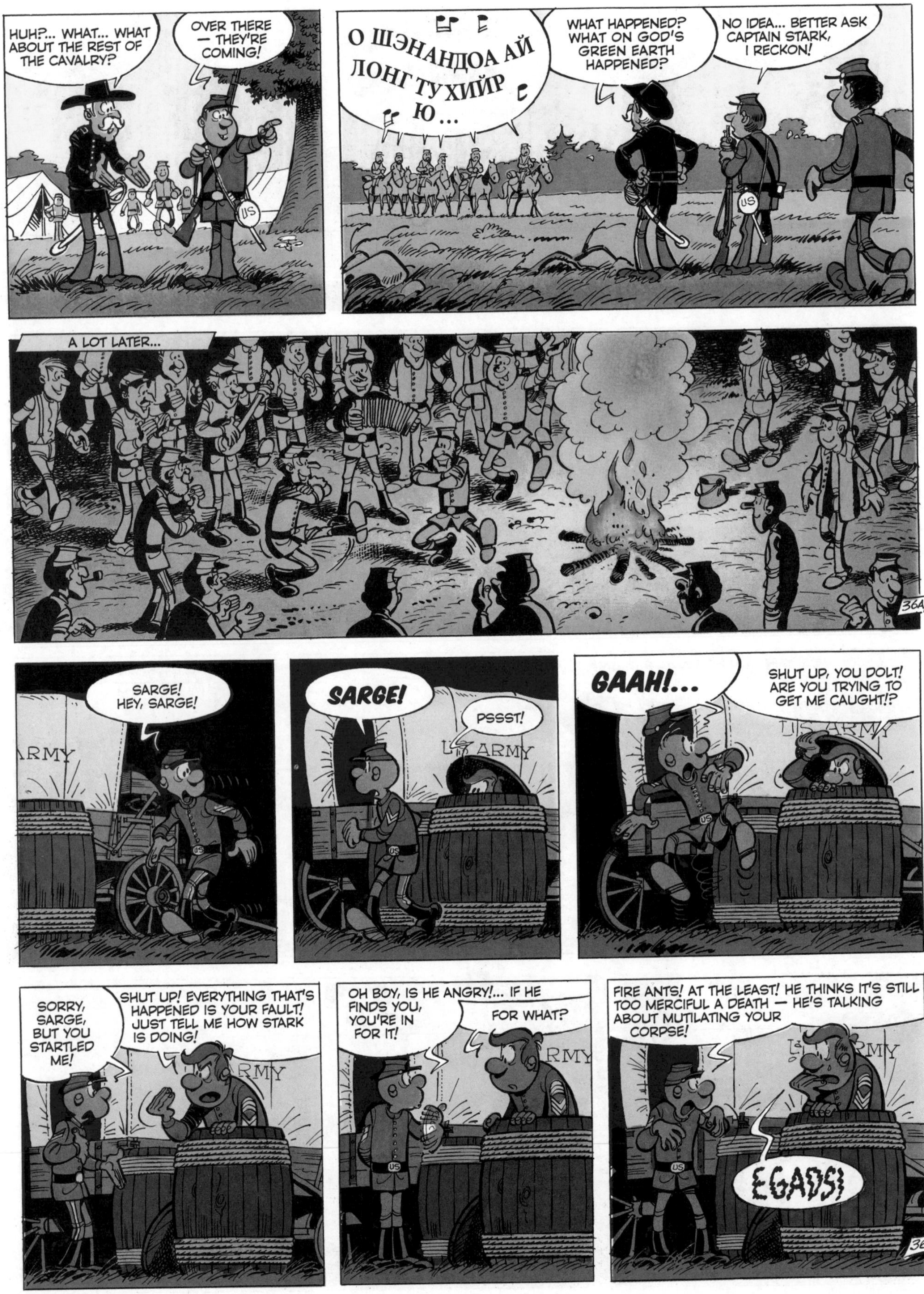

HUH?... WHAT... WHAT ABOUT THE REST OF THE CAVALRY?
OVER THERE — THEY'RE COMING!
О ШЭНАНДОА АЙ ЛОНГ ТУХИЙР Ю...
WHAT HAPPENED? WHAT ON GOD'S GREEN EARTH HAPPENED?
NO IDEA... BETTER ASK CAPTAIN STARK, I RECKON!
A LOT LATER...
36A
SARGE! HEY, SARGE!
SARGE!
PSSST!
GAAH!...
SHUT UP, YOU DOLT! ARE YOU TRYING TO GET ME CAUGHT!?
SORRY, SARGE, BUT YOU STARTLED ME!
SHUT UP! EVERYTHING THAT'S HAPPENED IS YOUR FAULT! JUST TELL ME HOW STARK IS DOING!
OH BOY, IS HE ANGRY!... IF HE FINDS YOU, YOU'RE IN FOR IT!
FOR WHAT?
FIRE ANTS! AT THE LEAST! HE THINKS IT'S STILL TOO MERCIFUL A DEATH — HE'S TALKING ABOUT MUTILATING YOUR CORPSE!
EGADS!
36B

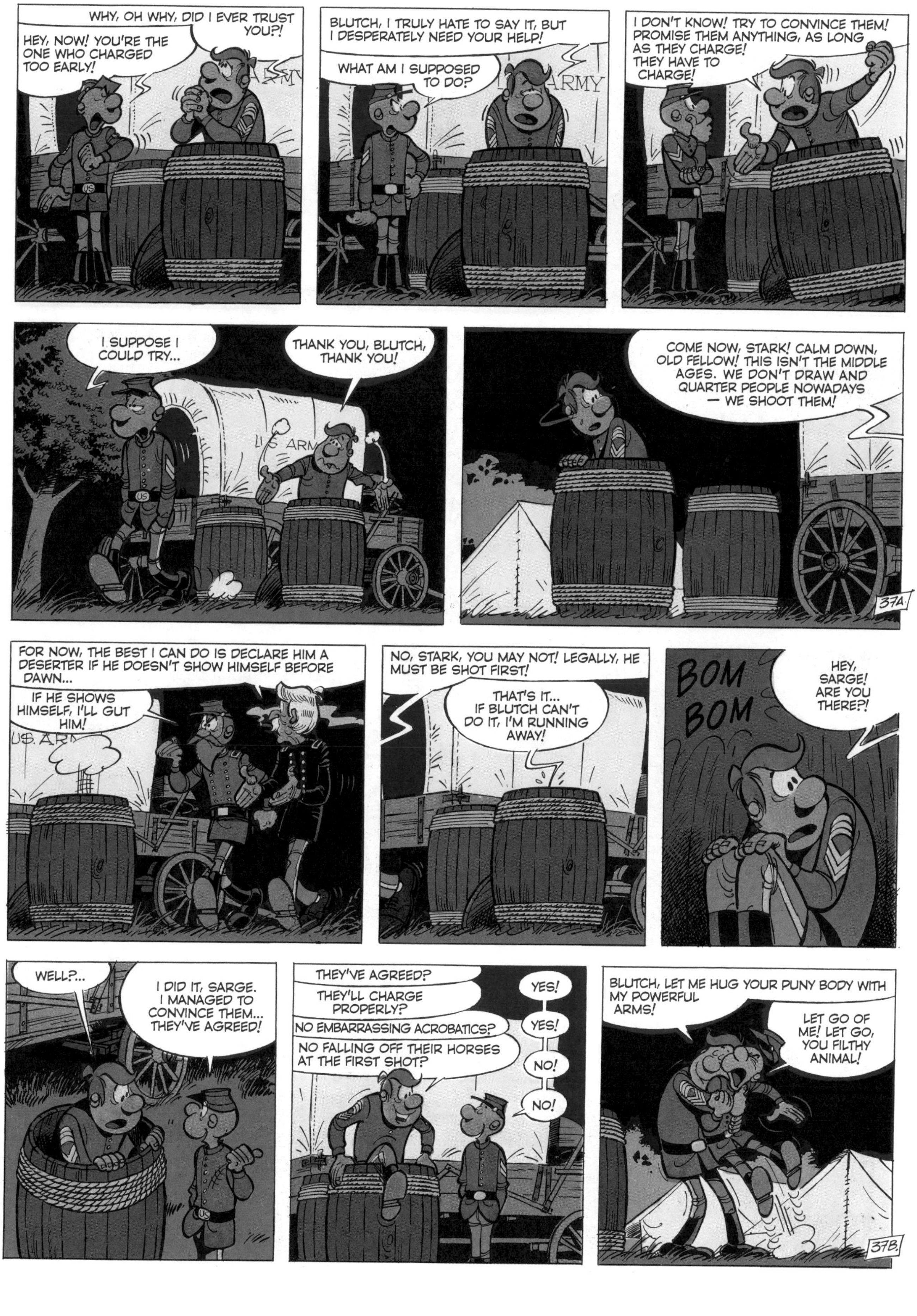
WHY, OH WHY, DID I EVER TRUST YOU?!
HEY, NOW! YOU'RE THE ONE WHO CHARGED TOO EARLY!
BLUTCH, I TRULY HATE TO SAY IT, BUT I DESPERATELY NEED YOUR HELP!
WHAT AM I SUPPOSED TO DO?
I DON'T KNOW! TRY TO CONVINCE THEM! PROMISE THEM ANYTHING, AS LONG AS THEY CHARGE! THEY HAVE TO CHARGE!
I SUPPOSE I COULD TRY...
THANK YOU, BLUTCH, THANK YOU!
COME NOW, STARK! CALM DOWN, OLD FELLOW! THIS ISN'T THE MIDDLE AGES. WE DON'T DRAW AND QUARTER PEOPLE NOWADAYS — WE SHOOT THEM!
37A
FOR NOW, THE BEST I CAN DO IS DECLARE HIM A DESERTER IF HE DOESN'T SHOW HIMSELF BEFORE DAWN...
IF HE SHOWS HIMSELF, I'LL GUT HIM!
NO, STARK, YOU MAY NOT! LEGALLY, HE MUST BE SHOT FIRST!
THAT'S IT... IF BLUTCH CAN'T DO IT, I'M RUNNING AWAY!
BOM BOM
HEY, SARGE! ARE YOU THERE?!
WELL?...
I DID IT, SARGE. I MANAGED TO CONVINCE THEM... THEY'VE AGREED!
THEY'VE AGREED?
YES!
THEY'LL CHARGE PROPERLY?
YES!
NO EMBARRASSING ACROBATICS?
NO!
NO FALLING OFF THEIR HORSES AT THE FIRST SHOT?
NO!
BLUTCH, LET ME HUG YOUR PUNY BODY WITH MY POWERFUL ARMS!
LET GO OF ME! LET GO, YOU FILTHY ANIMAL!
37B

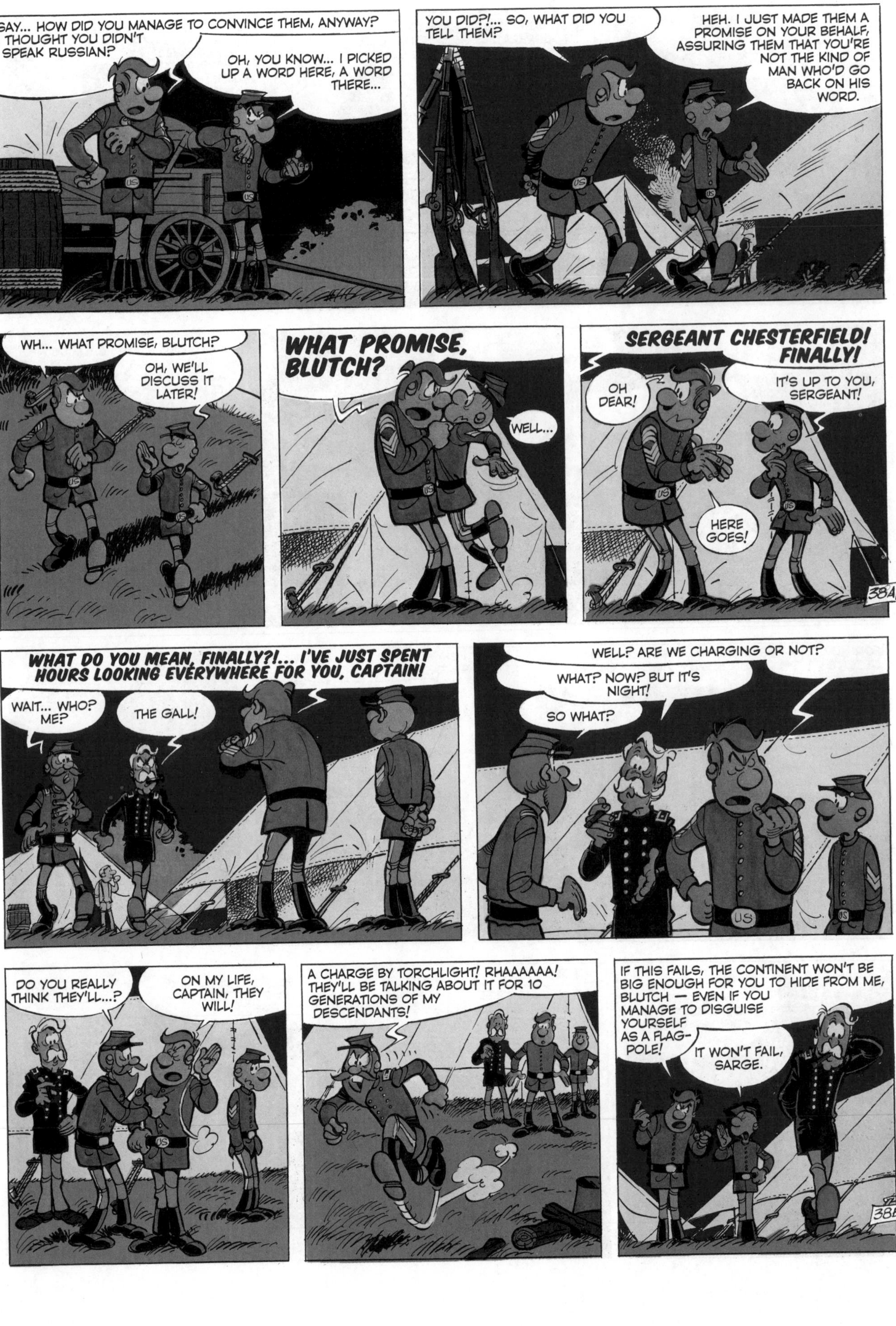
SAY... HOW DID YOU MANAGE TO CONVINCE THEM, ANYWAY? I THOUGHT YOU DIDN'T SPEAK RUSSIAN?
OH, YOU KNOW... I PICKED UP A WORD HERE, A WORD THERE...
YOU DID?!... SO, WHAT DID YOU TELL THEM?
HEH. I JUST MADE THEM A PROMISE ON YOUR BEHALF, ASSURING THEM THAT YOU'RE NOT THE KIND OF MAN WHO'D GO BACK ON HIS WORD.
WH... WHAT PROMISE, BLUTCH?
OH, WE'LL DISCUSS IT LATER!
WHAT PROMISE, BLUTCH?
WELL...
SERGEANT CHESTERFIELD! FINALLY!
OH DEAR!
IT'S UP TO YOU, SERGEANT!
HERE GOES!
38A
WHAT DO YOU MEAN, FINALLY?!... I'VE JUST SPENT HOURS LOOKING EVERYWHERE FOR YOU, CAPTAIN!
WAIT... WHO? ME?
THE GALL!
WELL? ARE WE CHARGING OR NOT?
WHAT? NOW? BUT IT'S NIGHT!
SO WHAT?
DO YOU REALLY THINK THEY'LL...?
ON MY LIFE, CAPTAIN, THEY WILL!
A CHARGE BY TORCHLIGHT! RHAAAAAA! THEY'LL BE TALKING ABOUT IT FOR 10 GENERATIONS OF MY DESCENDANTS!
IF THIS FAILS, THE CONTINENT WON'T BE BIG ENOUGH FOR YOU TO HIDE FROM ME, BLUTCH — EVEN IF YOU MANAGE TO DISGUISE YOURSELF AS A FLAG-POLE!
IT WON'T FAIL, SARGE.
38B

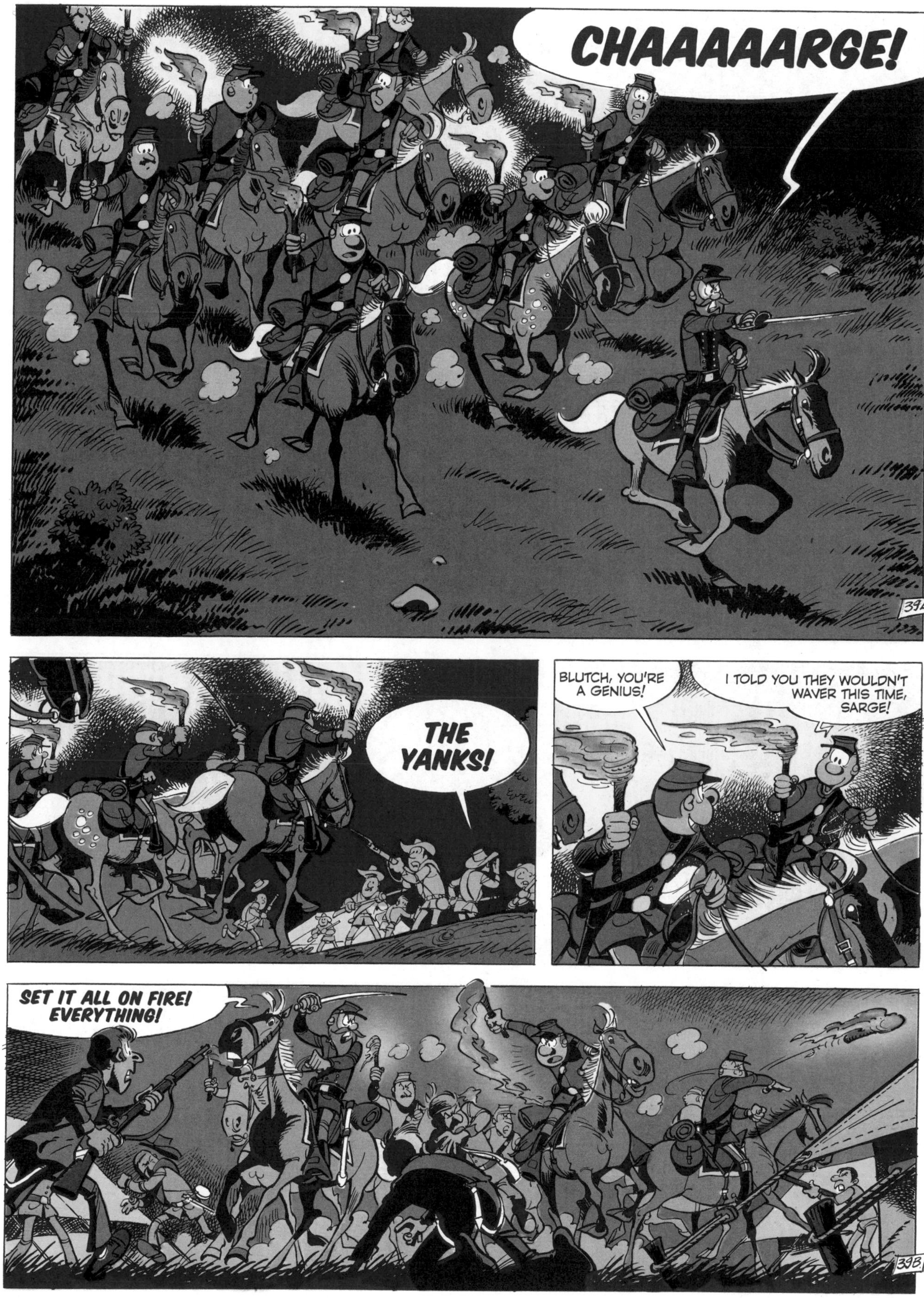
CHAAAAARGE!
THE YANKS!
BLUTCH, YOU'RE A GENIUS!
I TOLD YOU THEY WOULDN'T WAVER THIS TIME, SARGE!
SET IT ALL ON FIRE! EVERYTHING!

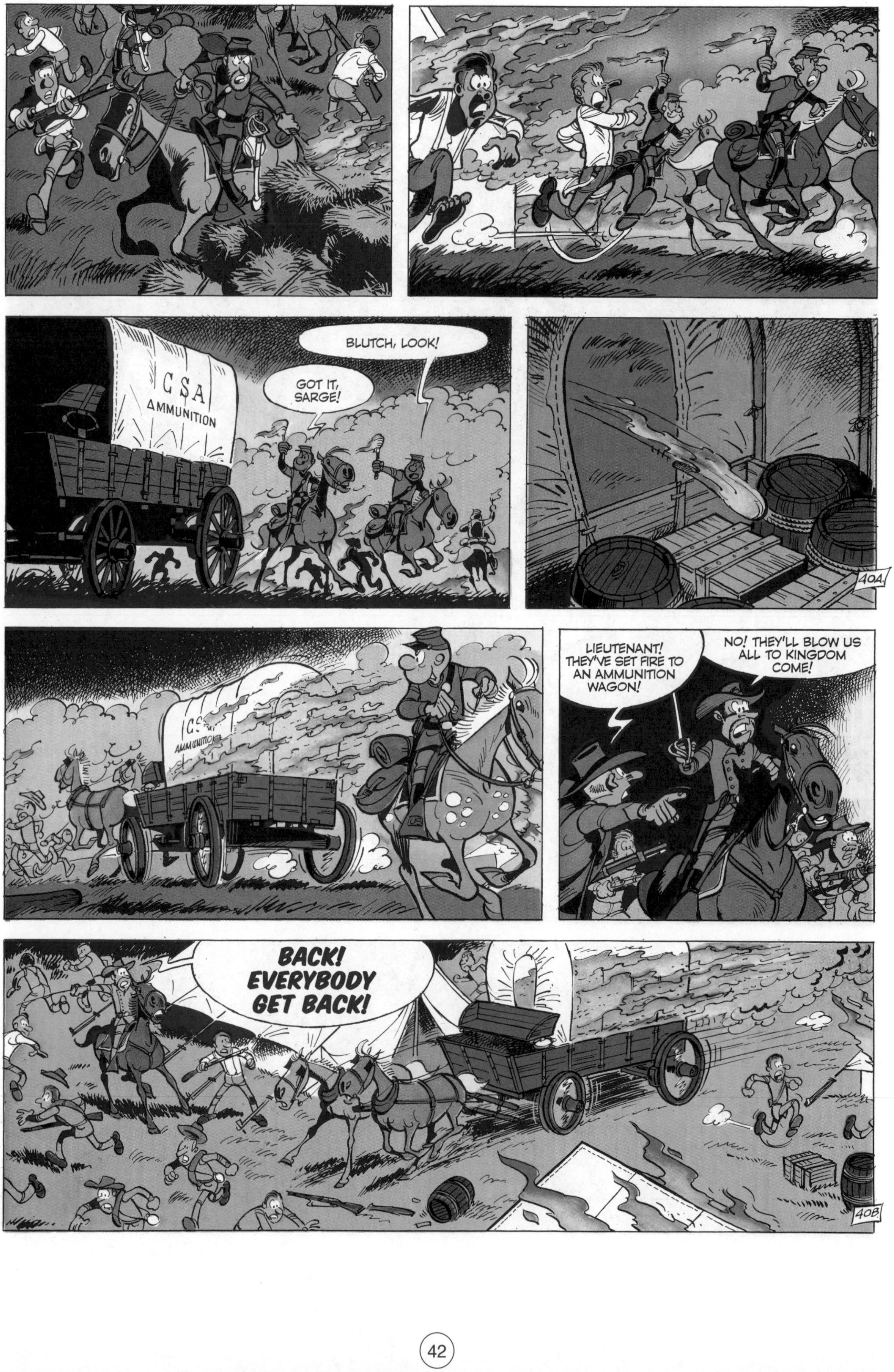
BLUTCH, LOOK!
GOT IT, SARGE!
CSA AMMUNITION
40A.
LIEUTENANT! THEY'VE SET FIRE TO AN AMMUNITION WAGON!
NO! THEY'LL BLOW US ALL TO KINGDOM COME!
BACK! EVERYBODY GET BACK!
40B

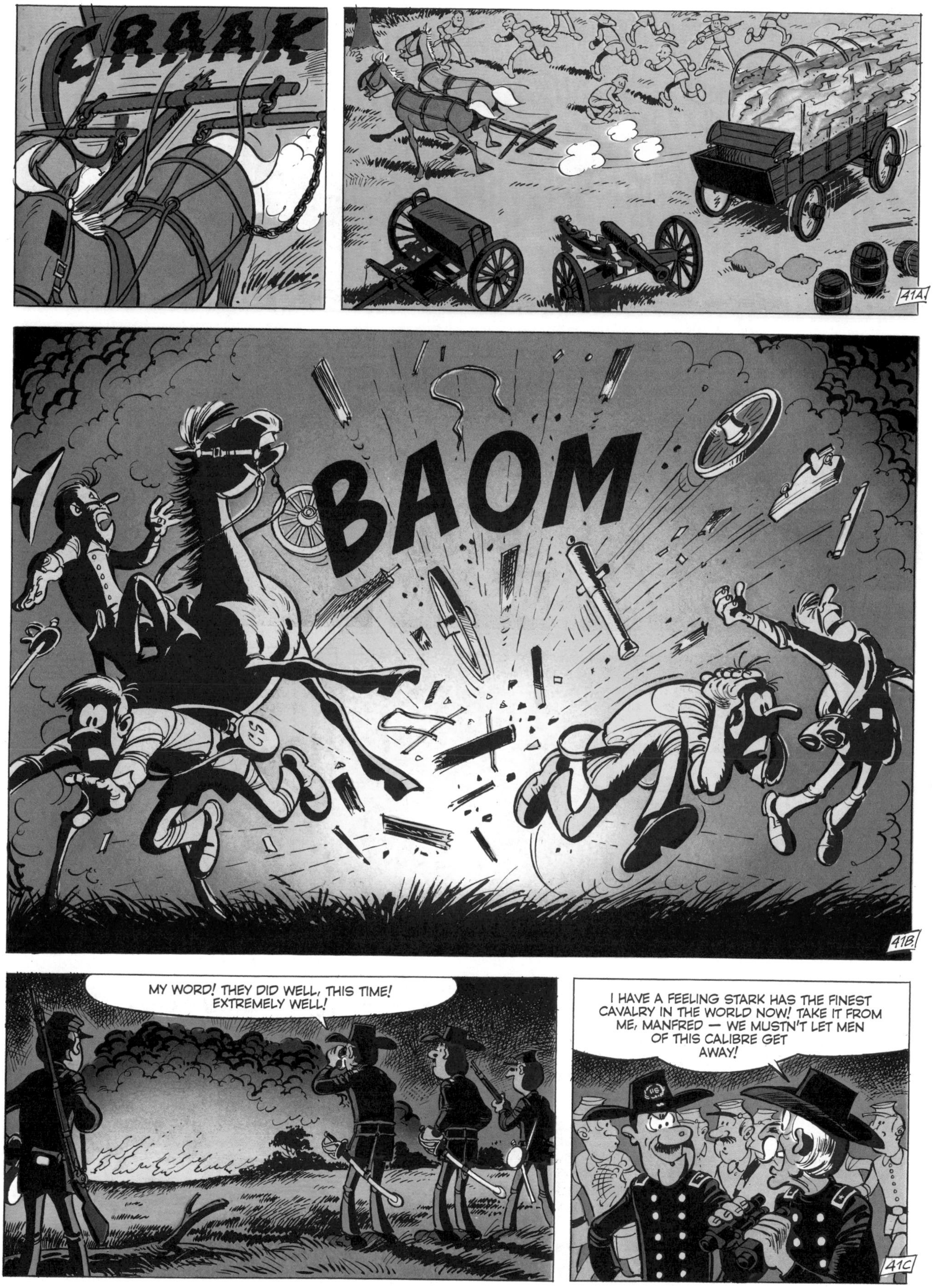
CRAAK
41A.
BAOM
41B.
MY WORD! THEY DID WELL, THIS TIME! EXTREMELY WELL!
I HAVE A FEELING STARK HAS THE FINEST CAVALRY IN THE WORLD NOW! TAKE IT FROM ME, MANFRED — WE MUSTN'T LET MEN OF THIS CALIBRE GET AWAY!
41C

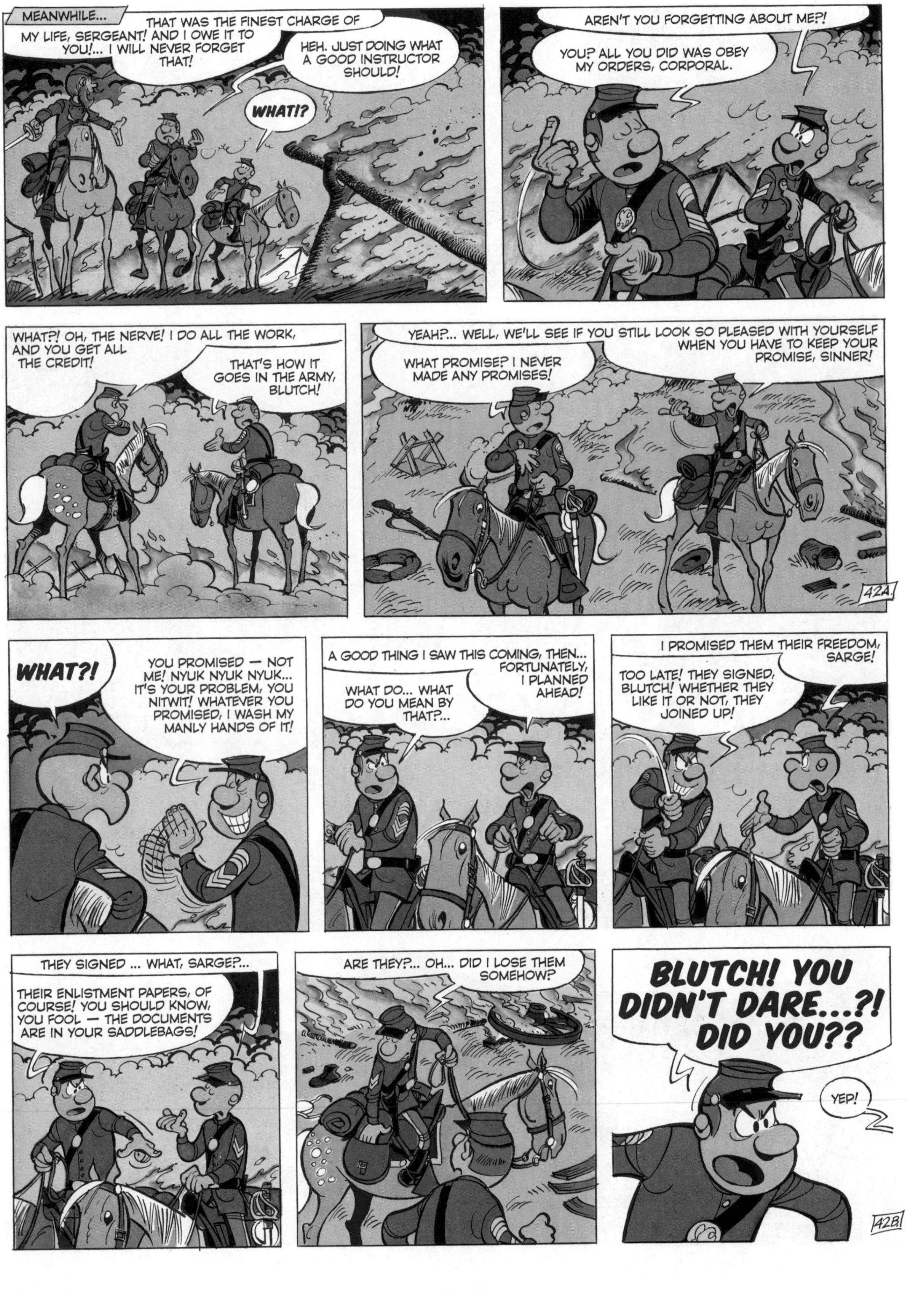
MEANWHILE...
THAT WAS THE FINEST CHARGE OF MY LIFE, SERGEANT! AND I OWE IT TO YOU!... I WILL NEVER FORGET THAT!
HEH. JUST DOING WHAT A GOOD INSTRUCTOR SHOULD!
WHAT!?
AREN'T YOU FORGETTING ABOUT ME?!
YOU? ALL YOU DID WAS OBEY MY ORDERS, CORPORAL.
WHAT?! OH, THE NERVE! I DO ALL THE WORK, AND YOU GET ALL THE CREDIT!
THAT'S HOW IT GOES IN THE ARMY, BLUTCH!
YEAH?... WELL, WE'LL SEE IF YOU STILL LOOK SO PLEASED WITH YOURSELF WHEN YOU HAVE TO KEEP YOUR PROMISE, SINNER!
WHAT PROMISE? I NEVER MADE ANY PROMISES!
42A.
WHAT?!
YOU PROMISED — NOT ME! NYUK NYUK NYUK... IT'S YOUR PROBLEM, YOU NITWIT! WHATEVER YOU PROMISED, I WASH MY MANLY HANDS OF IT!
A GOOD THING I SAW THIS COMING, THEN... FORTUNATELY, I PLANNED AHEAD!
WHAT DO... WHAT DO YOU MEAN BY THAT?...
I PROMISED THEM THEIR FREEDOM, SARGE!
TOO LATE! THEY SIGNED, BLUTCH! WHETHER THEY LIKE IT OR NOT, THEY JOINED UP!
THEY SIGNED ... WHAT, SARGE?...
THEIR ENLISTMENT PAPERS, OF COURSE! YOU SHOULD KNOW, YOU FOOL — THE DOCUMENTS ARE IN YOUR SADDLEBAGS!
ARE THEY?... OH... DID I LOSE THEM SOMEHOW?
BLUTCH! YOU DIDN'T DARE...?! DID YOU??
YEP!
42B

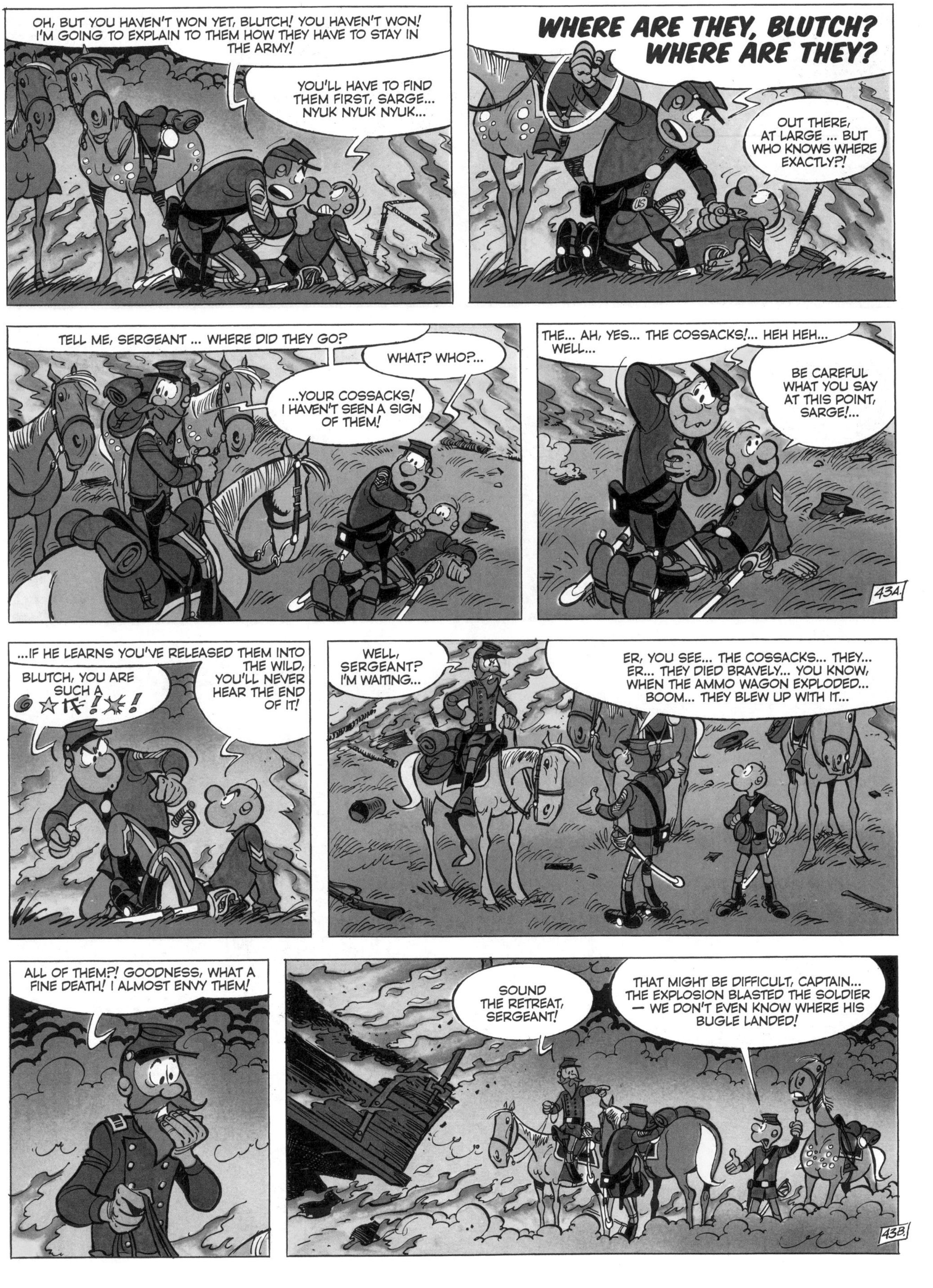
OH, BUT YOU HAVEN'T WON YET, BLUTCH! YOU HAVEN'T WON! I'M GOING TO EXPLAIN TO THEM HOW THEY HAVE TO STAY IN THE ARMY!
YOU'LL HAVE TO FIND THEM FIRST, SARGE... NYUK NYUK NYUK...
WHERE ARE THEY, BLUTCH? WHERE ARE THEY?
OUT THERE, AT LARGE ... BUT WHO KNOWS WHERE EXACTLY?!
TELL ME, SERGEANT ... WHERE DID THEY GO?
WHAT? WHO?...
...YOUR COSSACKS! I HAVEN'T SEEN A SIGN OF THEM!
THE... AH, YES... THE COSSACKS!... HEH HEH... WELL...
BE CAREFUL WHAT YOU SAY AT THIS POINT, SARGE!...
43A.
...IF HE LEARNS YOU'VE RELEASED THEM INTO THE WILD, YOU'LL NEVER HEAR THE END OF IT!
BLUTCH, YOU ARE SUCH A
WELL, SERGEANT? I'M WAITING...
ER, YOU SEE... THE COSSACKS... THEY... ER... THEY DIED BRAVELY... YOU KNOW, WHEN THE AMMO WAGON EXPLODED... BOOM... THEY BLEW UP WITH IT...
ALL OF THEM?! GOODNESS, WHAT A FINE DEATH! I ALMOST ENVY THEM!
SOUND THE RETREAT, SERGEANT!
THAT MIGHT BE DIFFICULT, CAPTAIN... THE EXPLOSION BLASTED THE SOLDIER — WE DON'T EVEN KNOW WHERE HIS BUGLE LANDED!
43B.

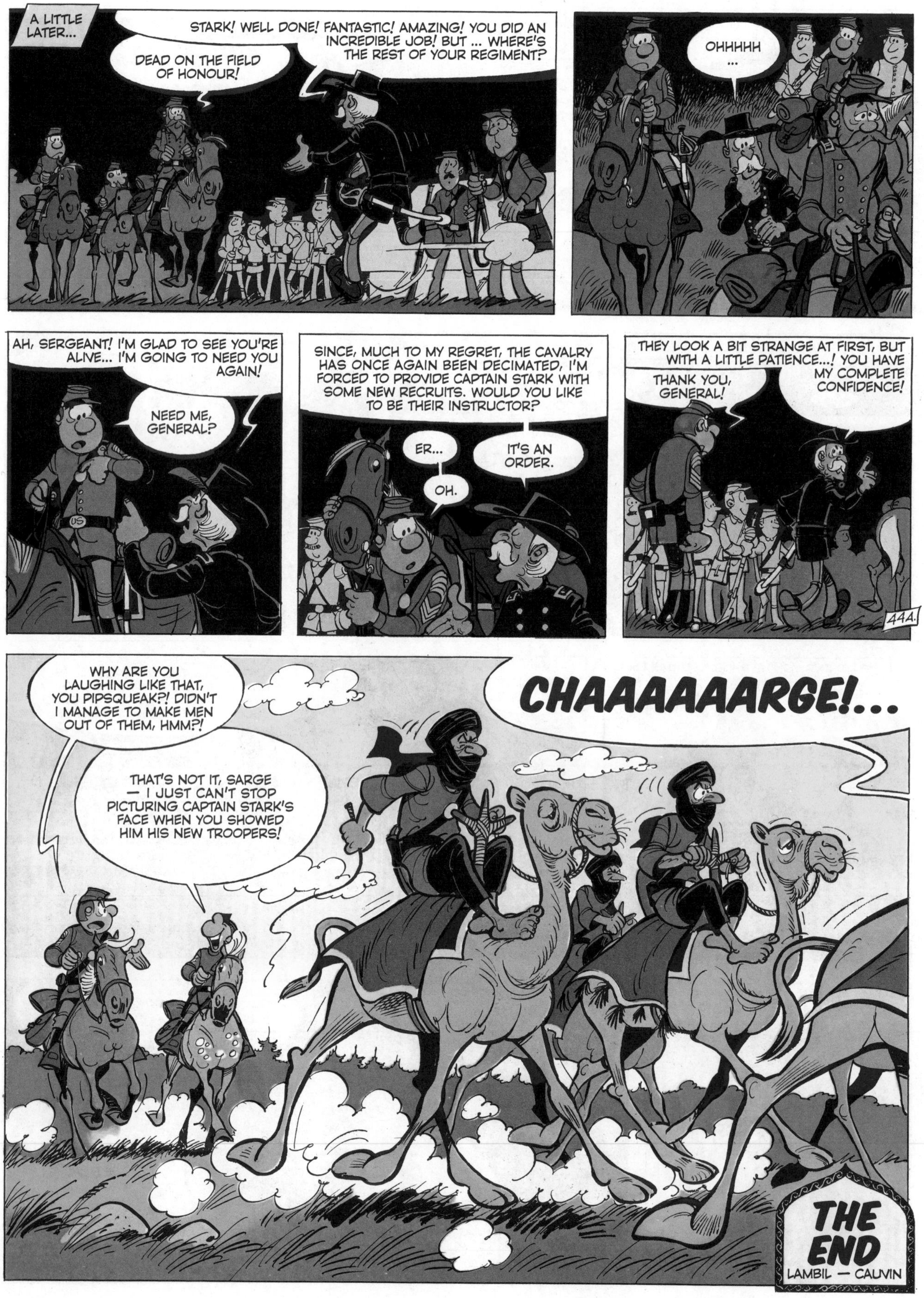

A LITTLE LATER...
STARK! WELL DONE! FANTASTIC! AMAZING! YOU DID AN INCREDIBLE JOB! BUT ... WHERE'S THE REST OF YOUR REGIMENT?
DEAD ON THE FIELD OF HONOUR!
OHHHHH ...
AH, SERGEANT! I'M GLAD TO SEE YOU'RE ALIVE... I'M GOING TO NEED YOU AGAIN!
NEED ME, GENERAL?
SINCE, MUCH TO MY REGRET, THE CAVALRY HAS ONCE AGAIN BEEN DECIMATED, I'M FORCED TO PROVIDE CAPTAIN STARK WITH SOME NEW RECRUITS. WOULD YOU LIKE TO BE THEIR INSTRUCTOR?
ER...
IT'S AN ORDER.
OH.
THEY LOOK A BIT STRANGE AT FIRST, BUT WITH A LITTLE PATIENCE...! YOU HAVE MY COMPLETE CONFIDENCE!
THANK YOU, GENERAL!
44A.
WHY ARE YOU LAUGHING LIKE THAT, YOU PIPSQUEAK?! DIDN'T I MANAGE TO MAKE MEN OUT OF THEM, HMM?!
THAT'S NOT IT, SARGE — I JUST CAN'T STOP PICTURING CAPTAIN STARK'S FACE WHEN YOU SHOWED HIM HIS NEW TROOPERS!
CHAAAAAAARGE!...
THE END
LAMBIL — CAUVIN

• THE BLUECOATS •

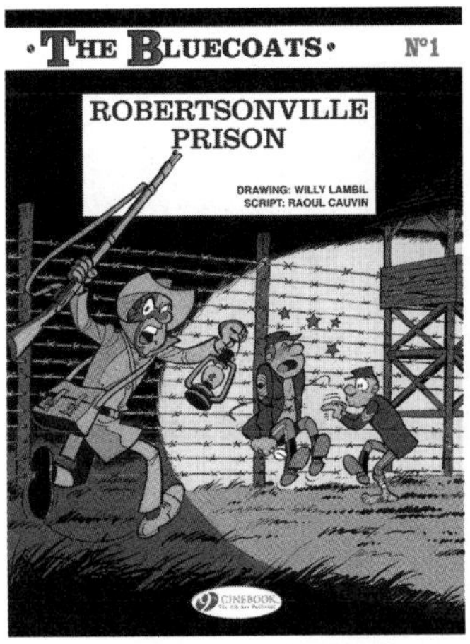
• THE BLUECOATS •
N°1
ROBERTSONVILLE PRISON
DRAWING: WILLY LAMBIL
SCRIPT: RAOUL CAUVIN

1 - ROBERTSONVILLE PRISON

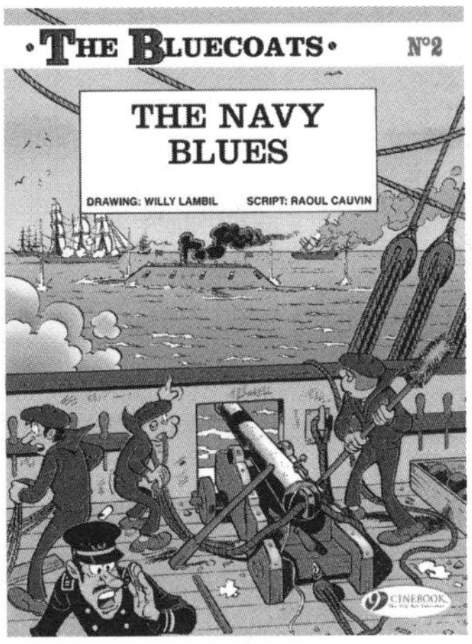
• THE BLUECOATS •
N°2
THE NAVY BLUES
DRAWING: WILLY LAMBIL SCRIPT: RAOUL CAUVIN

2 - THE NAVY BLUES

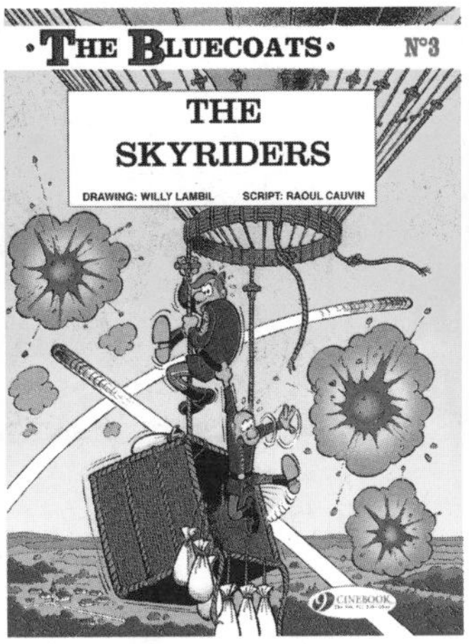
• THE BLUECOATS •
N°3
THE SKYRIDERS
DRAWING: WILLY LAMBIL SCRIPT: RAOUL CAUVIN

3 - THE SKYRIDERS

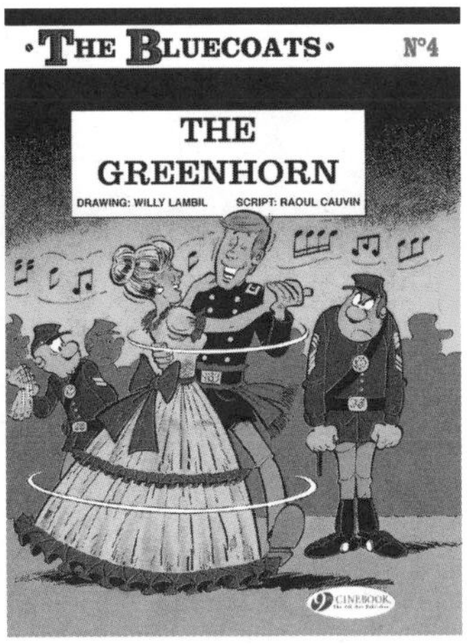
• THE BLUECOATS •
N°4
THE GREENHORN
DRAWING: WILLY LAMBIL SCRIPT: RAOUL CAUVIN

4 - THE GREENHORN

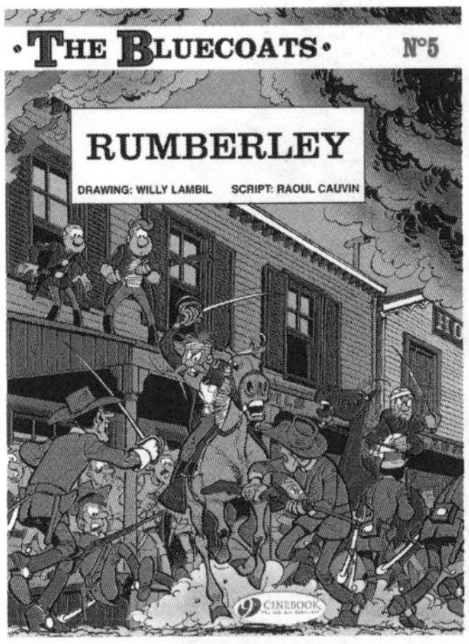
• THE BLUECOATS •
N°5
RUMBERLEY
DRAWING: WILLY LAMBIL SCRIPT: RAOUL CAUVIN

5 - RUMBERLEY

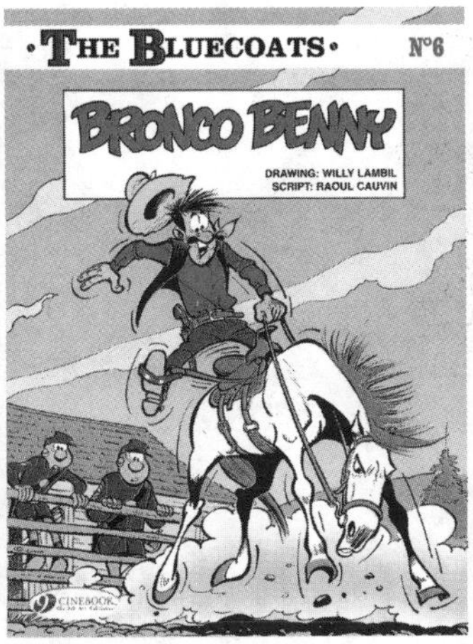
• THE BLUECOATS •
N°6
BRONCO BENNY
DRAWING: WILLY LAMBIL
SCRIPT: RAOUL CAUVIN

6 - BRONCO BENNY

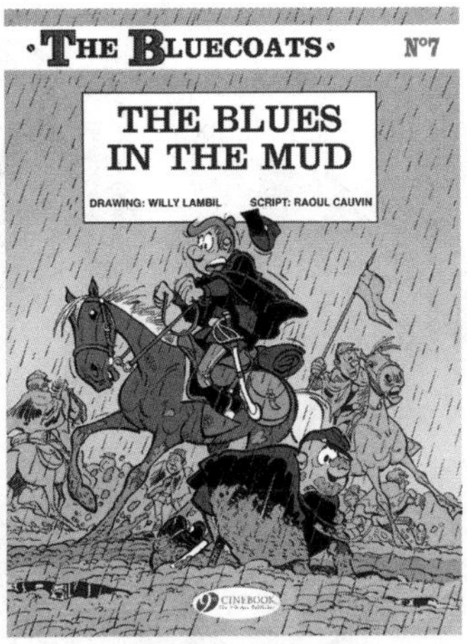
• THE BLUECOATS •
N°7
THE BLUES IN THE MUD
DRAWING: WILLY LAMBIL SCRIPT: RAOUL CAUVIN

7 - THE BLUES IN THE MUD

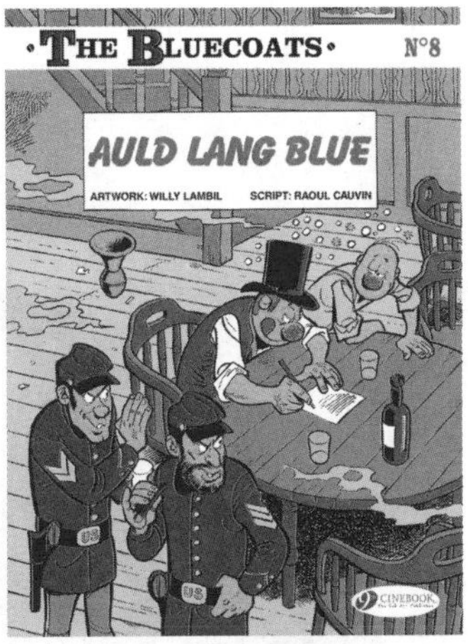
• THE BLUECOATS •
N°8
AULD LANG BLUE
ARTWORK: WILLY LAMBIL SCRIPT: RAOUL CAUVIN

8 - AULD LANG BLUE

COMING SOON

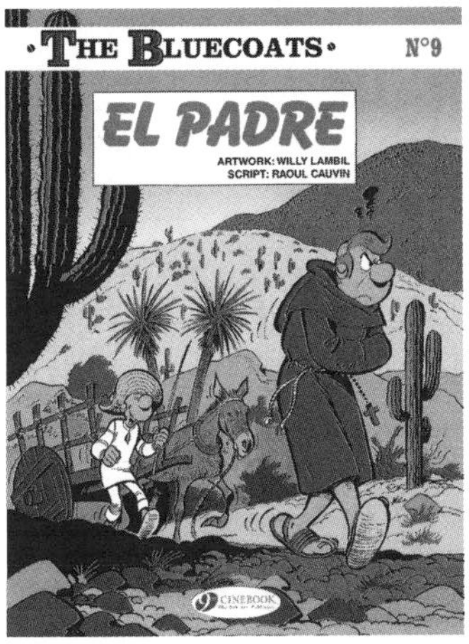
• THE BLUECOATS •
N°9
EL PADRE
ARTWORK: WILLY LAMBIL
SCRIPT: RAOUL CAUVIN

9 - EL PADRE

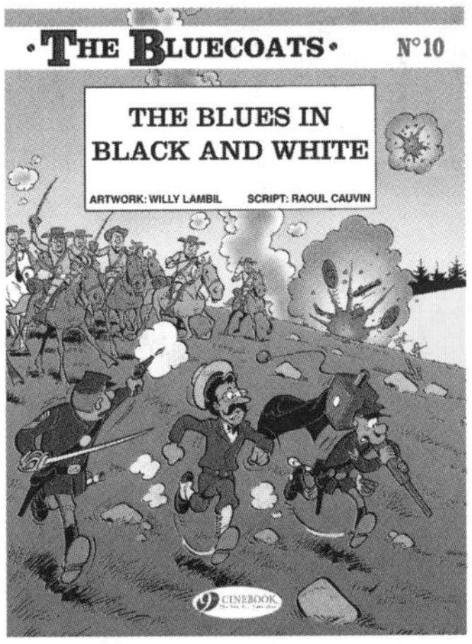
• THE BLUECOATS •
N°10
THE BLUES IN BLACK AND WHITE
ARTWORK: WILLY LAMBIL SCRIPT: RAOUL CAUVIN

10 - THE BLUES IN BLACK AND WHITE

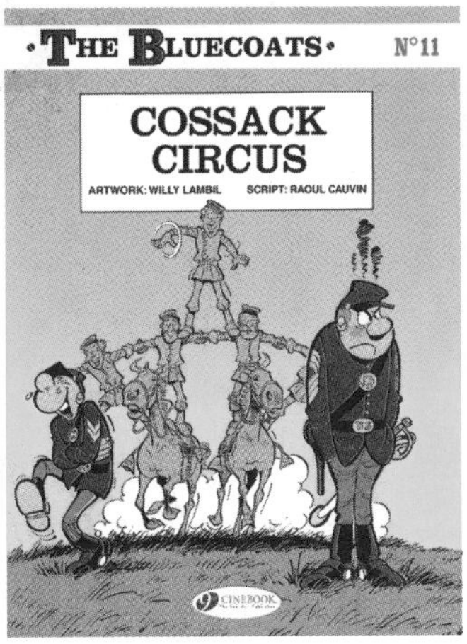
• THE BLUECOATS •
N°11
COSSACK CIRCUS
ARTWORK: WILLY LAMBIL SCRIPT: RAOUL CAUVIN

11 - COSSACK CIRCUS

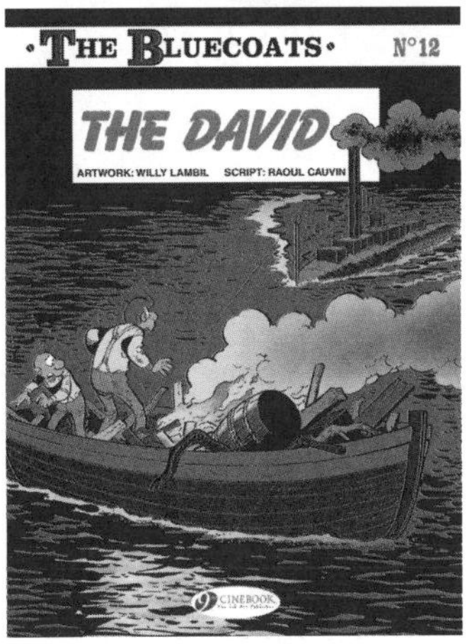
• THE BLUECOATS •
N°12
THE DAVID
ARTWORK: WILLY LAMBIL SCRIPT: RAOUL CAUVIN

12 - THE *DAVID*

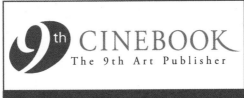